THE HALL OF FAME

FOR

GREAT AMERICANS

at New York University

COLONNADE: 181st Street and University Avenue

Executive Offices: 1009 Fifth Avenue
New York City

Ralph W. Sockman,
Director

Freda T. Hliddal,
Curator

OFFICIAL HANDBOOK

Edited by THEODORE MORELLO

NEW YORK UNIVERSITY PRESS

WASHINGTON SQUARE 1962

THE HALL OF FAME
FOR
GREAT AMERICANS

at **NEW YORK UNIVERSITY**

C=
2F
N567

DIRECTORS OF THE HALL OF FAME

Robert Underwood Johnson
SEPTEMBER, 1919 - OCTOBER, 1937

John H. Finley
DECEMBER, 1937 - MARCH, 1939

William Lyon Phelps
JANUARY, 1941 - AUGUST, 1943

James Rowland Angell
JANUARY, 1944 - MARCH, 1949

Ralph W. Sockman
JUNE, 1949 -

Henry Mitchell MacCracken, D.D., LL.D.

CHANCELLOR OF NEW YORK UNIVERSITY, 1891 - 1910

Originator and First Director of
The Hall of Fame for Great Americans

Let Us Now Praise Famous Men

Let us now praise Famous Men,
By whom the Lord hath wrought great glory.
Such as did bear rule in their kingdoms,
And were men renowned for their power,
Giving counsel by their understanding,
Such as have brought tidings in prophecies:
Leaders of the people by their counsels,
And by their understanding men of learning for the people;
Wise were their words in their instruction:
Such as sought out musical tunes,
And set forth verses in writing:
Men richly furnished with ability,
Living peaceably in their habitations:
All these were honored in their generations,
And were the glory of their times.
Yea, they were men of mercy,
Whose righteous deeds have not been forgotten.
Their bodies are buried in peace,
But their name liveth forevermore.
For the memorial of virtue is immortal;
Because it is known with God and with men.
When it is present, men take example of it;
And when it is gone, they desire it:
And throughout all time it marcheth crowned in triumph,
Victorious in the strife for the prizes that are undefiled.
Therefore will the people tell of their wisdom,
And the congregation will shew forth their praise.

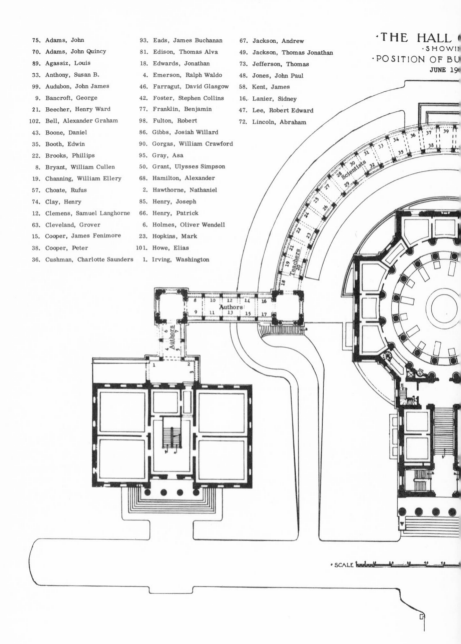

·THE HALL
·SHOWI
·POSITION OF BU
JUNE 19

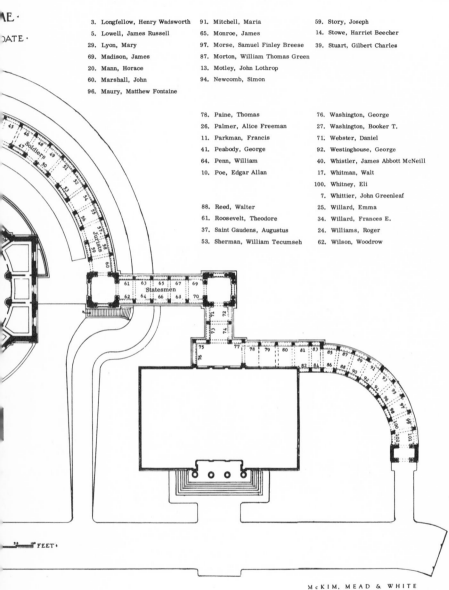

McKIM, MEAD & WHITE
Architects

Insignia and bookplate of the Hall of Fame
Wood Engraving by Timothy Cole
Original drawing by George Wharton Edwards

Introduction

WHEN THE HALL OF FAME for Great Americans was established more than 60 years ago, Dr. Henry M. MacCracken, then Chancellor of New York University, expressed the hope that the new institution would "teach youth that leaders in science and scholarship may be as great as military and naval heroes."

Dr. MacCracken, originator of the Hall of Fame, added: "The visitor to Washington finds in the Hall of Statuary, to which each State has been invited to contribute two statues of eminent citizens, that every man thus far honored, with a single eccentric exception, has been a holder of public office either military or civil. How different the result here, where out of the 29 names chosen [in the first quinquennial election] only 13 received their livelihood or their fame through the service of the State."

Through the decades since Dr. MacCracken spoke, the Hall of Fame has continued to add the names of distinguished Americans to its rolls until today 89 men and women are included in the august company. There are, of course, the names of military, political, and other public figures inscribed in the Hall of Fame— but they were not chosen lightly. In fact, only 12 United States Presidents have been so immortalized. The overwhelming majority of eminent Americans singled out were private citizens: poets, novelists, educators, theologians, reformers, scientists, or painters. Thus has history supported Dr. MacCracken's conviction that greatness may be attained in many walks of life.

CONTENTS

Names Honored in the Hall of Fame

APPENDICES

ALPHABETICAL LISTING OF NAMES HONORED

At the Hall of Fame for Great Americans on May 13, 1924
Thomas Alva Edison unveiled the bust of Joseph Henry, inventor
of the electromagnet and first head of the Smithsonian Institution.

Edison himself was elected to the Hall of Fame in 1960. The
bronze bust was unveiled June 4, 1961.

STORY OF

The Hall of Fame for Great Americans

IT IS FITTING that the Hall of Fame for Great Americans should stand on ground prominent in Revolutionary history. Designed by Stanford White, the celebrated architect, and financed by a gift from Mrs. Finley J. Shepard (Helen Gould), the edifice is situated on the campus of New York University on University Heights. The eminence, with its commanding view of the Harlem and Hudson River Valleys and the craggy Palisades beyond, was occupied at its highest point by the center of the British army in the successful attack upon Fort Washington.

The principal architectural feature of the Hall of Fame is the open-air Colonnade, 630 feet long. It rests upon a massive granite substructure which has been designated as a museum. The graceful, curving Colonnade wherein are displayed the bronze busts of great Americans was dedicated officially on May 30, 1901.

New York University holds title to the Hall of Fame and administers it through its Senate. Nevertheless, the University regards itself as merely a trustee of this national, patriotic, and educational shrine that belongs to all the people of the United States.

The process of selection of the first candidates for enshrinement began early in 1900, when the public was invited to submit nominations. Provisions were made to include up to 50 names in the initial election.

By May 1, 1900, more than 1,000 nominations had been received by the New York University Senate. Having designated some 100 prominent persons throughout the country as electors, the Senate submitted to them the 100 names which had received the greatest public support. To this number were added 100 nominees selected by the Senate. The electors themselves were invited to suggest other candidates. The final list contained a total of 234 names from which 29 were elected by the required majority vote.

Eight names were added in 1905, ten in 1910, nine in 1915, seven in 1920, two in 1925, four in 1930, three in 1935, one in 1940, four in 1945, six in 1950, three in 1955, and three in 1960, bringing to 89 the total number elected.

Under the original constitution governing the Hall of Fame, no foreign-born citizen was eligible for election. To rectify this obvious injustice, the University Senate in 1904 decided to establish a Hall of Fame for foreign-born Americans. However, in 1914 the constitution was changed to strike out any distinction between native citizens and Americans of foreign birth.

One alien has been granted what might be considered "associate membership": in recognition of the Marquis de Lafayette's service in the American Revolution, his bust occupies a special niche in the wall of an adjacent University building. From there the statue of the French soldier and statesman overlooks the Colonnade where—but for an accident of birth—the bronze image would stand today.

Also in 1914, the University set apart a site in the Colonnade for a Hall of Fame for Women. But eight years later, after seven names had been chosen, the University Senate decided to abolish in future elections any discrimination as to sex and to combine the names of the women with those of the men. Today, the Colonnade displays the bronze likenesses of eight women.

In 1922, the required period of time between the death of a prospective candidate and his eligibility for election was increased from ten years to 25 years.

It was a basic concept of its founders that the Hall of Fame be national rather than regional in character. To this end, the minimum number of electors has been fixed at 100, with all states represented. As Dr. Henry Mitchell MacCracken, originator of the Hall of Fame and at that time New York University's Chancellor, observed in 1901: "Local and temporary influence or the solicitations of interested supporters are not likely to weigh seriously with a tribunal so constituted." Today, approximately 140 electors represent all 50 states.

From the list of nominees submitted to them by the University Senate, the electors may choose a maximum of seven persons for admission to the Hall of Fame. Later, a committee of leading American artists selects an outstanding sculptor who will execute a bronze bust of each winning candidate. The bust must be made specifically for the Hall of Fame and must not be duplicated for exhibition elsewhere within 50 years of its execution.

The considerable cost of enshrinement, including the unveiling ceremony, is usually borne by private citizens or institutions dedicated to perpetuating the memory of the dignitary elected.

Looking to the future, the Hall of Fame plans, when funds become available, to establish a museum of letters, books, portraits, and other mementos of the Americans whose names it has inscribed. The six rooms and long corridor which constitute the ground story of the Hall of Fame are to be set aside for this purpose.

If the site of a British military victory as the locale for an institution dedicated to America's most distinguished men and women seems paradoxical, consider the words of Dr. MacCracken, who said of University Heights:

"Lost to the invaders in 1776, this summit is now retaken by the goodly troop of 'Great Americans,' General Washington their leader. They enter into possession of these Heights and are destined to hold them, we trust, forever."

Constitution

Adopted 1900: Amended 1904, 1914, 1920, 1922, 1944, and 1945.

ONE

The Senate of New York University shall appoint the Electors of the Hall of Fame, shall conduct the quinquennial elections, and shall be empowered to make and amend the Rules for Elections, subject to the Conditions of the Gift and to this Constitution.

TWO

The Electors of the Hall of Fame shall consist of approximately one hundred persons appointed for a five-year term or until their successors are appointed. In the appointments due recognition shall be given to geographical distribution and vocational classification.

THREE

Elections to the Hall of Fame shall be held every five years.

FOUR

Panels for bronze tablets in the "Hall of Fame for Great Americans" shall be filled as follows: Fifty names may be inscribed in 1900, provided fifty shall be approved in accordance with the Constitution and Rules for Elections. At the close of every five years thereafter five additional names may be inscribed, until the entire number of panels shall have been filled.

FIVE

Should the full number thus authorized not be inscribed at any quinquennial election, the Senate may approve the choice of more than five, but not to exceed seven names at any succeeding election, provided those so elected in addition to those previously chosen shall not exceed the cumulative total which Rule Four makes possible at the completion of each quinquennial election.

SIX

Election to the Hall of Fame shall require an affirmative vote of a majority of the entire body of Electors.

SEVEN

The Senate of New York University, acting by a majority of its voting members, shall have the power to disapprove the choice of any name.

EIGHT

No name may be inscribed except of a person whose home was in the United States and who has been deceased at least twenty-five years.

NINE

The Senate shall determine an appropriate classification of citizens by vocation or achievement, and shall assign each name chosen for inscription in the Hall of Fame to its proper class.

Rules for Elections

ONE

The Electors of the Hall of Fame, consisting of approximately one hundred persons, shall be appointed by the Senate of New York University, in approximately equal numbers, from the following seven groups of citizens, and shall be so classified: 1] Actual or former University or College Executives; 2] Historians or Professors of History or Literature; 3] Scientists; 4] Authors, Editors and Artists; 5] Men and Women of Affairs; 6] Actual or former High Public Officials; 7] Actual or former Justices, National or State.

TWO

Every State or group of adjacent States having approximately one million inhabitants shall be given one Elector. No person connected with New York University shall be eligible as an Elector.

THREE

The Director of the Hall of Fame shall invite the public to submit names to be considered by the duly constituted authorities for commemoration in the Hall of Fame.
Such names may be presented from April 1 preceding the election to April 1 of the election year. Such nominations from the general public must be submitted on forms obtainable from the office of the Director.

FOUR

All names received from the public shall be placed before the Senate of New York University, and every name seconded by a member of the Senate shall be placed upon a preliminary list of nominations which shall be sent on or about April 15 of the election year to the Committee on Nominations provided for in Section Six.

FIVE

The Senate shall assign each name upon the preliminary list of nominations to one of the following sixteen classes:

1] Authors (Editors, Poets, Novelists, Philosophers, Economists, etc.).
2] Educators.
3] Preachers, Theologians.
4] Reformers.
5] Scientists.
6] Engineers, Architects.
7] Physicians, Surgeons.
8] Inventors.
9] Missionaries, Explorers.
10] The Military.
11] Lawyers, Judges.
12] Statesmen.
13] Business Men, Philanthropists.
14] Artists (Musicians, Painters, Sculptors, Actors, etc.).
15] Naturalists.
16] Men and Women outside the foregoing classes.

SIX

A Committee on Nominations consisting of three Electors from each of the divisions of Electors provided for in Section One shall be designated by the Senate. To this Committee of Twenty-one shall be submitted all names upon the preliminary list of nominations, on or about April 15.

SEVEN

The Committee on Nominations shall be requested to canvass this preliminary list and to indicate for their colleagues on the Electoral College those names which are deemed worthy of special consideration. This list is to be returned to the Director of the Hall of Fame not later than May 10 of the election year.

EIGHT

All names which have been placed in nomination shall be placed upon the final ballot, with the votes of the members of the Committee on Nominations indicated thereon. Also, all candidates presented in a previous election who have received 20 or more votes shall automatically become eligible for consideration at the next election.

NINE

The final ballot, containing the list of nominations for the election, shall be sent to each Elector on or about June 1 of the election year.

TEN

Each Elector shall be requested to mark, sign and mail to the Director of the Hall of Fame the final ballot by October 1 following. Each name judged worthy to be inscribed in the Hall of Fame shall be marked thus (x), before the name. When an Elector fails to submit a ballot, this failure is regarded as a resignation from the College of Electors.

ELEVEN

Votes must be received before October 15.

TWELVE

Elections to the Hall of Fame shall require an affirmative vote of a majority of the entire body of Electors.

THIRTEEN

Each name thus approved will be inscribed in the Hall of Fame unless disapproved before November 1 by a majority of the voting members of the Senate.

Names Honored in the
Hall of Fame for Great Americans

I
AUTHORS

GEORGE BANCROFT, statesman and historian, was born in Worcester, Mass., October 3, 1800, and died in Washington, D.C., January 17, 1891. His capacity for learning so impressed the Harvard faculty that when he was graduated at the age of 16, college officials raised funds to send him to Germany to study. He received his doctor of philosophy degree from Gottingen at the age of 19 and was a pupil of Hegel in Berlin. Though trained in the German school of dispassionate historiography, Bancroft showed his deep feeling for the young republic in his ten-volume history of the United States. He was a keen partisan in the events of his century and early in life rejected Federalism to further the cause of Jacksonian democracy. As Secretary of the Navy under President Polk, he was instrumental in founding the Naval Academy at Annapolis. He ordered seizure of Mexican gunboats in California and, as acting Secretary of War, sent General Zachary Taylor across the Texas border —acts which led directly to the Mexican War. Bancroft was official eulogist at memorial rites for two Presidents: Lincoln, whom he had supported on the slavery issue, and Andrew Jackson. During his service as Minister to Great Britain and later to Germany, he collected important information about the American Revolution from British and German as well as French archives. He also used his influence in order to pry new facts from letters, diaries, and other private papers. His *History of the United States,* the first volume of which appeared in 1834, was not completed for nearly half a century. An honor in which he took particular pride was his election as the 17th—and only Anglo-Saxon—member of the *Mittwochs-Gesellschaft für Wissenschaftliche Unterhaltung,* a society of 16 German savants.

History interposes with evidence that tyranny and wrong lead inevitably to decay; that freedom and right, however hard may be the struggle, always prove resistless.

George Bancroft

[ELECTED IN 1910 BY 53 VOTES]

BUST by Rudulph Evans; unveiled May 8, 1930; gift of Officers of the Navy, active or retired, through the efforts of Captain C. H. Harlow, U.S.N. [Ret.], and of members of the American Historical Association and others; unveiled by Professor Wilder D. Bancroft of Cornell University, grandson of the historian; address prepared by Hon. David Jayne Hill, former American Ambassador to Germany, read by Professor Evarts B. Greene, President of the American Historical Association and Professor of American History at Columbia.

So live that when thy summons comes . . .
Thou go not like the quarry slave at night
Scourged to his dungeon, but, sustained
and soothed
By an unfaltering trust, approach thy grave
Like one who wraps the drapery of his
couch
About him, and lies down to pleasant
dreams.

William Cullen Bryant

[ELECTED IN 1910 BY 59 VOTES]

BUST by Herbert Adams; unveiled May 9, 1929; gift of Cyrus H. K. Curtis, for the New York Evening Post; unveiled by the poet's grandson, Harold Godwin; address by Dr. Wilbur L. Cross, Dean of the Graduate School, Yale University, and member of the American Academy of Arts and Letters.

WILLIAM CULLEN BRYANT, poet and editor, was born at Cummington, Mass., November 3, 1794, and died in New York City, June 12, 1878. His first home was a farmhouse set amid apple orchards, fields, and forests. In these surroundings the precocious boy's talents ripened quickly. His masterpiece, *Thanatopsis*, was written when he was 17, but it was stuffed into a desk and forgotten. Bryant struggled to prepare himself for Yale until his father broke the news that no funds were available. He turned to law and was admitted to the bar in 1815. He wrote *To a Waterfowl* when, supremely discouraged, he walked over to the village of Plainfield to set up law practice. On the way he saw against a red sky a single bird in flight. *Thanatopsis* was discovered when his father looked in his desk after being prodded by Willard Phillips, an editor of the *North American Review,* to find any manuscript William might have to contribute. The poem made such an impression that one editor doubted that anyone "on this side of the Atlantic is capable of writing such verse." Four years after its publication in 1817 Bryant was invited to read the Phi Beta Kappa poem at the Harvard commencement. This original poem, *The Ages,* was published with *Green River, To a Waterfowl,* and *The Yellow Violet* in 1821. Bryant's most prolific years were 1824 and 1825, when he produced *Rizpah, Monument Mountain,* and more than 20 other poems. After moving to New York, he spent a year coediting a magazine and nearly half a century as co-owner and coeditor of the *Evening Post.* During this time he published new collections, among them *The Fountain, and Other Poems* (1842) and in 1878, the year of his death, *The Flood of Years* and *A Lifetime.*

SAMUEL LANGHORNE CLEMENS [Mark Twain], humorist and author, was born in Florida, Mo., November 30, 1835, and died in Redding, Conn., April 21, 1910. In 1839 the family moved to Hannibal, Mo., a town which later was to become the home of the legendary Tom Sawyer and his friends. Clemens received little formal education, but learned the printing trade early in life on the Hannibal newspaper. Later, he worked as an itinerant printer on newspapers in St. Louis, Philadelphia, and New York. Subsequently, he was a Mississippi river pilot, a miner in Nevada, and a newspaper reporter in San Francisco. He was reporting the Nevada constituent convention for the Virginia City *Enterprise* when he first began to sign his dispatches "Mark Twain," a river pilot's cry indicating water two fathoms deep. It was also while he was in the West that he heard the campfire tale he later molded into *The Celebrated Jumping Frog of Calaveras County*. It won immediate popularity upon being published in the New York periodical, *The Saturday Press*, on November 18, 1865. Two years afterward, the tale gave its name to his first book, a series of sketches. Letters written during a trip to Europe and the Middle East provided material for *The Innocents Abroad* (1869), which within five years had sold 150,000 copies. Following his marriage to Olivia Langdon, he described his Western adventures in *Roughing It* (1872), and recounted his river life in *Old Times on the Mississippi* (1883). *The Adventures of Tom Sawyer* (1876) and *The Adventures of Huckleberry Finn* (1884) are generally considered his best works. Yet this master of robust humor was a romanticist, too. His historical novel *The Prince and the Pauper* (1880) was followed by *A Connecticut Yankee in King Arthur's Court* (1889) and *Personal Recollections of Joan of Arc* (1896).

Loyalty to petrified opinion never yet broke a chain or freed a human soul.

Samuel Langhorne Clemens [Mark Twain]

[ELECTED IN 1920 BY 72 VOTES]

BUST by Albert Humphreys; unveiled May 13, 1924; gift of the Estate of Mark Twain; unveiled by his daughter, Mrs. Ossip Gabrilowitsch; address by Miss Agnes Repplier.

I now feel mortified and grieved when I meet with an American gentleman who professes anything but liberal opinions as respects the rights of his fellow-creatures.

James Fenimore Cooper

[ELECTED IN 1910 BY 62 VOTES]

BUST by Victor Salvatore; unveiled May 8, 1930; gift of a friend of the Hall of Fame on behalf of the Museum of the American Indian; unveiled by Dr. Henry S. Fenimore Cooper, great-grandson of the novelist; address by Dr. John Erskine, Professor of English at Columbia.

JAMES FENIMORE COOPER, novelist, was born in Burlington, N. J., September 15, 1789, and died in Cooperstown, N. Y., September 14, 1851. He spent his boyhood in the family's baronial wilderness mansion at Cooperstown, which his father had founded. Following dismissal from Yale in his third year, he spent five years at sea, from which he retired in 1811 to marry and to become a country gentleman. Nearly a decade later an accident started him on his literary career. While reading a novel, he boasted to his wife that he could write a better one. When she challenged him to try, he produced *Precaution* (1820), an undistinguished novel. But it was *The Spy* (1821), with its flight and pursuit, its suspense, and vigorous narrative style, which set the pattern for novels that were to follow. An instant success, *The Spy* was presented as a stage drama in New York and translated into French only months after publication. By the time *The Pioneers* and *The Pilot* appeared two years later, Cooper had become a literary personage. From these he moved on to *The Last of the Mohicans* (1826) and *The Prairie* (1827), romanticized accounts of Daniel Boone's life. He took his family to France in 1826 and traveled widely in Europe for five years. His return to New York marked the beginning of bitter feuds with his critics, litigations, and declining popularity. Still, he managed to produce his scholarly *The History of the Navy of the United States of America* (1839) and, in the two succeeding years, two more of his Leatherstocking Tales, *The Pathfinder* and *The Deerslayer*. A fresh burst of creative energy produced books on such disparate themes as Spain in Columbus' time, the pre-Revolutionary British Navy, and the fashionable life of Manhattan.

RALPH WALDO EMERSON, poet and essayist, was born in Boston, May 25, 1803, and died at Concord, Mass., April 27, 1882. His father, a clergyman of the First Unitarian Church, died when Ralph was eight. He struggled through Harvard and was graduated as class poet at the age of 18. Incipient tuberculosis interrupted his studies at Harvard Divinity School. After regaining his health in the South, he accepted the pastorate of the Old North (Second Unitarian) Church in Boston in 1829. In the same year he married Ellen Tucker; 17 months later his bride died of tuberculosis. In 1832 he resigned his pastorate and broke with the ministry because of his honest doubts on points of Unitarian doctrine. Free now to pursue a literary career, he sailed for Europe for a period of philosophical study. There he met Carlyle, Coleridge, and Wordsworth. Returning home, he married Lydia Jackson in 1835; published his first book, *Nature* (1836); and began his association with Thoreau, Margaret Fuller, and other transcendentalists, who believed that God was inherent in all nature and that man should fulfill himself according to his individual beliefs. In 1838 he addressed the Harvard Divinity School in the famous lecture in which he declared that man must look for salvation within himself. As a result of the storm that followed his unorthodox stand, he was *persona non grata* at Harvard for nearly 30 years; it wasn't until 1866 that the college relented so far as to award him an LL.D. degree. Meanwhile, his fame as a lecturer grew. He published a number of essays, followed by his first volume of poetry, *Poems*, in 1846 and his second, *May-Day and Other Pieces*, 21 years later. His other published works included *English Traits, Addresses and Lectures, Representative Men,* and *Conduct of Life.*

The day is always his who works in it with serenity and great aims. The unstable estimates of men crowd to him whose mind is filled with the truth as the heaped waves of the Atlantic follow the moon.

Ralph Waldo Emerson

[ELECTED IN 1900 BY 87 VOTES]

BUST by Daniel Chester French; unveiled May 22, 1923; gift of the Authors' Club of Boston; unveiled by Dr. Edward Waldo Emerson, son of the poet; address by Dr. Henry van Dyke.

Living in solitude till the fulness of time,
I still kept the dew of my youth and the
freshness of my heart.

Nathaniel Hawthorne

[ELECTED IN 1900 BY 73 VOTES]

BUST by Daniel Chester French; unveiled May 9, 1929; gift of L. Brooks Leavitt, a Bowdoin alumnus of the class of 1899; unveiled by Miss Una Hawthorne Deming, great-granddaughter of the novelist; address by Dr. William Lyon Phelps, Professor of English at Yale University, read by Major Curtis Hidden Page.

NATHANIEL HAWTHORNE, novelist and short-story writer, was born in Salem, Mass., July 4, 1804, and died at Plymouth, N. H., May 19, 1864. His most famous novel, *The Scarlet Letter*, illustrates the brooding preoccupation with sin of early Puritan society. The son of a ship's captain, he spent 12 years at home with his widowed mother after his graduation from Bowdoin College in 1825. During those years he supported himself by writing magazine articles. He also finished an unsuccessful, anonymous novel, *Fanshawe*. In 1842 he married Sophia Peabody, a member of the Emerson-Thoreau circle. He and his bride established residence in Concord where Hawthorne produced *Mosses from an Old Manse*. Later, in Salem, he wrote *The Scarlet Letter*, published in 1850. While working on short stories (*Twice-Told Tales*), novels, and journalistic articles, he pieced out his income by accepting civil appointments, first as a measurer at the Boston customhouse and later as surveyor of the port at Salem. He lived for a time on the "Tanglewood" estate near Lenox, Mass., where he met Herman Melville and wrote *The House of the Seven Gables* (1851). *The Blithedale Romance* was written the following year. In 1852 he wrote a campaign biography which aided in the election of one of his college mates, Franklin Pierce, to the U.S. presidency. Hawthorne was rewarded by an appointment as U.S. Consul in Liverpool. During his stay abroad he visited Italy and finished one novel, *The Marble Faun*. His experience in the consular service also produced *Our Old Home*, a series of satirical sketches about England. Back in the United States, he took a trip to the White Mountains with Pierce. It was on this trip that Hawthorne died at Plymouth. He was buried at Concord.

OLIVER WENDELL HOLMES, essayist, poet, and teacher of anatomy, was born in Cambridge, Mass., August 29, 1809, and died in Boston, October 7, 1894. After graduation from Harvard College in 1829 he made his first appearance as a writer of verse in the periodicals *Collegian* and *Amateur*. *Old Ironsides*, printed in the *Boston Daily Advertiser* of September 16, 1830, brought him his first wide recognition and was instrumental in saving the frigate "Constitution" from destruction. In 1831 an article appeared in the *New England Magazine* titled *The Autocrat of the Breakfast Table*, a forerunner of the famous series which appeared in the *Atlantic Monthly* from 1857 to 1891. This series, later published in book form, included *The Autocrat at the Breakfast Table*, which contains *The Chambered Nautilus* and *The Deacon's Masterpiece; or The Wonderful One-Hoss Shay* — respectively masterpieces of his serious and lighter verse. After studying medicine in Boston and Paris he received his medical degree from Harvard in 1836 and began practicing in Boston. But he made his mark in the field chiefly as a writer on medical subjects and as a teacher of anatomy. He published two medical pamphlets, *Homeopathy and Its Kindred Delusions* and *The Contagiousness of Puerperal Fever*, both of which still are regarded as milestones in medical research. He spoke well and was widely sought after as a lecturer on both medical and literary topics. He subsequently turned to the novel, producing *Elsie Venner*, *The Guardian Angel*, and *A Mortal Antipathy*. The year after his death his verse was published in the Cambridge Edition of *The Complete Poetical Works of Oliver Wendell Holmes*, a 300-page volume. He was the father of the great Supreme Court Justice of the same name.

Build thee more stately mansions, O my soul,
As the swift seasons roll!
Leave thy low-vaulted past!

Oliver Wendell Holmes

[ELECTED IN 1910 BY 69 VOTES]

BUST by Edmond T. Quinn; unveiled May 9, 1929; gift of a group of friends of Dr. Holmes; unveiled by Edward J. Holmes, grandson of the poet; address by Dr. John H. Finley, Associate Editor of the New York Times, and member of the American Academy of Arts and Letters; singing by Madame Louise Homer of "The Last Leaf," set to music by Sidney Homer.

The intercourse between the author and his fellowmen is ever new, active, and immediate. Well may the world cherish his renown. It has been purchased by the diligent dispensation of pleasure.

Washington Irving

[ELECTED IN 1900 BY 83 VOTES]

BUST by Edward McCartan; unveiled May 5, 1927; gift of The Hispanic Society of America; presented by Hon. John Bassett Moore, Vice-President of the Society and Judge of the Permanent Court of International Justice; unveiled by Alexander Duer Irving, great-great-nephew of the historian; addresses by Royal Cortissoz of the American Academy of Arts and Letters and His Excellency Señor Don Alejandro Padilla y Bell, Royal Spanish Ambassador.

WASHINGTON IRVING, essayist and historian, was born in New York City, April 3, 1783, and died at Tarrytown, N.Y., November 28, 1859. Although known chiefly for his droll accounts of Dutch villages on the Hudson River, Irving was also a serious historical biographer of Columbus and George Washington, among others. Besides several European journeys which earned him fame on both sides of the Atlantic, Irving visited the American frontier where he gathered material for *A Tour on the Prairies,* published in 1835, and *The Adventures of Captain Bonneville, U.S.A.* (1837). His boyhood schooling had been fragmentary. In 1798 he entered a law firm, where he seems to have spent much of his leisure time writing sketches about the society and theater of New York. *The Letters of Jonathan Oldstyle, Gent.* was published in 1802. Worried about his health, his brothers underwrote an extensive European tour for him in 1804. After his return two years later he joined in publishing *Salmagundi,* a series of humorous and satirical essays that mirrored New York social life. He followed this with "Diedrich Knickerbocker's" *A History of New York,* in 1809. That year also brought personal tragedy; Irving's fiancée died. The death so shocked him that he remained unmarried to the end of his life. At this point the family hardware business began to deteriorate, and, although he went to England to try to strengthen the Liverpool branch, the entire firm failed. Thereupon Irving turned definitely to literature. *The Legend of Sleepy Hollow, Rip Van Winkle,* and other essays appeared serially in New York in 1819–20 and were published as *The Sketch Book of Geoffrey Crayon, Gent.* in 1820.

SIDNEY LANIER, poet, was born in Macon, Ga., February 3, 1842, and died at Lynn, N.C., September 7, 1881. His mother was an accomplished musician, which probably accounts for his early musical tendencies. In his youth he learned to play the piano, the violin, the flute, the guitar, and the organ. While at Oglethorpe College, from which he was graduated in 1860, he learned to play the banjo. In 1861 he entered the Confederate Army and emerged at the end of the war with his health impaired. During this period he turned his energy to writing verse. The bulk of his verse, prose, and music was created between 1865 and 1879, when he was appointed lecturer in English literature at Johns Hopkins University. Virtually all of Lanier's works were produced under the greatest difficulties; he was nearly always ill, often destitute, and frequently both. In 1873 he joined the Peabody Symphony Orchestra in Baltimore as first flutist. A ten-volume edition of his life and letters, edited by Charles R. Anderson and published by The Johns Hopkins University Press, encompasses everything that Lanier created. Among his poems perhaps his most widely known are *Song of the Chattahoochee, The Marshes of Glynn, A Ballad of Trees and the Master, The Centennial Meditation of Columbia,* and *Sunrise.* A discriminating treatise on poetry and music is contained in his volume of prose, *Science of English Verse.* Among his musical compositions are "Danse des Moucherons," "Love That Hath Us in the Net," "Field Larks and Blackbirds," "Swamp Robin," and "Wind Song." The poem *Sunrise,* written on his deathbed, is filled with such beauty as to suggest that, had he lived longer, he might easily have ranked with the highest in the arts.

Weakness, in freedom, grows stronger than strength with a chain.

Sidney Lanier

[ELECTED IN 1945 BY 48 VOTES]

BUST by Hans Schuler; unveiled October 3, 1946; gift of the United Daughters of the Confederacy; The Foster Hall Collection of the University of Pittsburgh, and Mr. Stephen J. Wigmore; formal presentation by Mrs. John M. Wilcox, President-General, United Daughters of the Confederacy; unveiled by Sidney Lanier, grandson of the poet. A tribute to Lanier was delivered by Dr. Isaiah Bowman, President of The Johns Hopkins University, and an address was made by Mrs. Walter D. Lamar, Chairman, Sidney Lanier Committee, United Daughters of the Confederacy. Music by Jean Dickenson and John Wummer, solo flute, The Philharmonic Symphony Orchestra of New York.

The distant mountains that uprear
  Their lofty bastions to the skies
Are crossed by pathways that appear
  As we to higher levels rise.

The heights by great men reached and kept
  Were not attained by sudden flight,
But they, while their companions slept,
  Were toiling upward in the night.

Henry Wadsworth Longfellow

[ELECTED IN 1900 BY 85 VOTES]

BUST by Rudulph Evans; unveiled May 9, 1929; gift of a friend of the Hall of Fame on behalf of the American Academy of Arts and Letters; unveiled by Miss Mary Dana, Longfellow's great-granddaughter; address by Dr. Richard Burton; sonnet, written for the occasion, by Major Curtis Hidden Page, President of the Poetry Society of America.

HENRY WADSWORTH LONGFELLOW, poet, was born in Portland, Me., February 27, 1807, and died at Cambridge, Mass., March 24, 1882. His poems turned American historical incidents, heroes, and legends into sagas of almost mythological importance. As a young man Longfellow admired Washington Irving, and, like Irving, began his career with frequent transatlantic voyages. Tragedy struck on his second trip when his wife died at Rotterdam in 1835. He continued his tour alone for a while but returned in 1836 to occupy the chair of modern languages and belles-lettres at Harvard. There followed a period of intense creative activity; he wrote The Wreck of the Hesperus, Excelsior, The Village Blacksmith, and many other poems. In 1843 he married Frances Appleton, the real-life heroine of his prose romance, Hyperion. Some of his most notable poems belong to this period, including Evangeline, The Courtship of Miles Standish, The Song of Hiawatha, and Paul Revere's Ride. In 1861 the second Mrs. Longfellow died in a fire. Fifty years after his graduation from Bowdoin College, he again attended commencement exercises, this time to recite from the podium his Morituri Salutamus, a statement of the mingled weakness and strength of old age. In that half-century he had succeeded in winning world-wide recognition for American poetry. He had learned ten languages, become a distinguished professor and scholar, and translated Dante's Divine Comedy. His home at Cambridge, "Craigie House," had become a mecca of literary pilgrimages. However, the supreme tribute came when Longfellow's bust was placed in the Poets' Corner of Westminster Abbey; he was the first American to be accorded that distinction.

JAMES RUSSELL LOWELL, author, teacher, and public servant, was born in Cambridge, Mass., February 22, 1819, and died in the same house, "Elmwood," August 12, 1891. He received his bachelor's degree from Harvard College in 1838 and was graduated from Harvard Law School in 1840. His public debut as a poet came in 1841 with the appearance of *A Year's Life.* Antislavery sentiments expressed in *Poems* (1844) reflected the influence of Maria White whom he married that year. *The Changeling* and *She Came and Went* commemorated poetically the death in infancy of their first child, just as the volume *The Poems of Maria Lowell* memorialized his wife's death in 1853. The midcentury saw publication of *Poems by James Russell Lowell, Second Series, A Fable for Critics, The Vision of Sir Launfal,* and the first volume of *The Biglow Papers.* The last is illustrative of his writing skill, wit, and devotion to liberty. In 1855 in Boston he delivered at Lowell Institute a lecture series on English poets. Later, he was appointed a Harvard professor of languages and belles-lettres. In 1857 he became editor of the *Atlantic Monthly,* first published that November. The editorship gave Lowell, Emerson, Hawthorne, and other significant writers an outlet for vigorous expression and exerted a powerful influence on public taste. *Ode Recited at the Harvard Commemoration, July 21, 1865,* written in memory of Harvard's Civil War dead, represents Lowell at his best. Prose writing and public service dominated his later years. He was successively a delegate to the Republican National Convention, an Electoral College member, and U.S. Minister to Spain and to England. In 1885 he returned to private life.

*No power can die that ever wrought for
    Truth;
Thereby a law of nature it became
And lives unwithered in its blithesome
    youth
When he who calls it forth is but a name.*

James Russell Lowell

[ELECTED IN 1905 BY 59 VOTES]

BUST by Allan Clark; unveiled May 8, 1930; gift of a friend of the Hall of Fame on behalf of the American Academy of Arts and Letters; unveiled by James Russell Lowell, great-grandson of the poet; address by Dr. William Lyon Phelps, Professor of English at Yale University.

I venture to hope that the lovers of human progress and the admirers of disinterested virtue may find encouragement in the deep-taled history of an heroic people in its most eventful period.

John Lothrop Motley

[ELECTED IN 1910 BY 51 VOTES]

JOHN LOTHROP MOTLEY, historian and diplomat, was born at Dorchester, Mass., April 15, 1814, and died in Dorset, England, May 29, 1877. The son of a wealthy Boston family, he attended the Round Hill School at Northampton, Mass., where one of his teachers was George Bancroft, the historian. Motley was graduated from Harvard at the age of 17. He studied in Germany and later made the grand tour of Europe, during which he met Bismarck and translated Goethe's *Faust* into English. After returning to Boston he married Mary Benjamin. He wrote two novels and spent one term in the Massachusetts legislature before deciding on a career as a historian. He is chiefly remembered as the author of *The Rise of the Dutch Republic*, a book which he wrote three times—once in the United States, once in Germany, and once in Holland. When it was published at his own expense in 1856, Motley expected sales of only about 100 copies. Instead, there was an immediate and heavy demand which justified a second edition within a year. Some 17,000 copies were sold in England and the same number in the United States. Reviewers called it a picturesque, dramatic narrative and a brilliant personal interpretation of history. During his diplomatic career Motley was stationed briefly in St. Petersburg and later became U.S. Minister to Austria (1861–67) and to Great Britain (1869–70). At these posts his access to national archives allowed him to gather historical material for his books. He also wrote *The History of the United Netherlands* and *The Life and Death of John of Barneveld*. The parallel between Dutch and American independence struggles attracted him to the Netherlands, where he lived for some time in a house set apart for him in The Hague by the Queen. He died and was buried in England.

BUST by Frederick MacMonnies; May 8, 1930; gift of a friend of the Hall of Fame on behalf of the National Institute of Arts and Letters; unveiled by Master John Lothrop Motley, Jr., great-great-nephew of the historian; address prepared by Hon. David Jayne Hill, historian and diplomat, read by Dr. John H. Finley.

THOMAS PAINE, political theorist and writer, was born at Thetford, England, January 29, 1737, and died in New York City, June 8, 1809. Although his formal schooling ended when he was 13, he continued to read widely and developed a keen interest in science. Fired by the American colonists' struggle for freedom, he came to America and, as editor of the *Pennsylvania Magazine*, gave expression in print to his democratic ideals. His pamphlet, *Common Sense*, published anonymously, appeared in 1776. In the same year he published his first *Crisis*, a periodical which was followed by eleven other issues during the Revolution. The series was of inestimable value in raising patriotic morale. The following year he was appointed secretary to the congressional committee on foreign affairs. Later, he raised funds in France for General Washington's army. At the end of the war, Paine found himself covered with glory but almost penniless. However, the State of Pennsylvania gave him £500, and New York deeded him a farm at New Rochelle. In 1787 he returned to England where his *Rights of Man* was published. It was suppressed by the British; and Paine, who had fled to France, was tried *in absentia* for treason. In appreciation of his espousal of democracy, the French awarded him citizenship and elected him to the French Convention, but political changes threw him into disfavor. He was stripped of French citizenship and cast into prison, where he wrote *The Age of Reason.* Released through the efforts of James Monroe, then the American Minister, he returned to the United States. Ill and poor, he found himself in disrepute because of his attacks on the Bible and on Washington. He died virtually ostracized. Nevertheless, to the very end, his influence remained strong among a small but loyal following.

Those who expect to reap the blessings of freedom, must, like men, undergo the fatigues of supporting it. . . .

Thomas Paine

[ELECTED IN 1945 BY 51 VOTES]

BUST by Malvina Hoffman; unveiled May 18, 1952; gift of the Thomas Paine National Historical Association of New Rochelle, New York. In addition to the principal fund, a few contributions were received from friends of Paine. Formal presentation by Mr. Henry M. Lester, President, Thomas Paine National Historical Association; unveiled by Mr. Edward W. Stitt, Jr., Vice-President, Thomas Paine National Historical Association and City Historian of New Rochelle, New York. Address by Dr. Wesley Frank Craven, Edwards Professor of American History, Princeton University.

The narrator must seek to imbue himself with the life and spirit of the time. He must himself be, as it were, a sharer or a spectator of the action he describes.

Francis Parkman

[ELECTED IN 1915 BY 68 VOTES]

BUST by Hermon A. MacNeil; unveiled May 9, 1929; gift of a friend of the Hall of Fame on behalf of the Museum of the American Indian, Heye Foundation; unveiled by the historian's granddaughter, Mrs. James H. Perkins; address by Dr. Edward Channing, Professor of History at Harvard University and member of the American Academy of Arts and Letters.

FRANCIS PARKMAN, historian, was born in Boston, Mass., September 16, 1823, and died there November 8, 1893. He was steeped in the traditions of Boston and had an intense interest in early American history. By the time he had become a sophomore at Harvard he already had chosen the topic that was to become his life work: the history of the Anglo-French conflict in North America. In 1846, after finishing Harvard Law School, he went on a seven-month expedition over the Oregon and Santa Fe Trails to obtain first-hand knowledge of the Indians. For a time he lived among them and became adept at woodcraft, riding, and shooting. Though afflicted with poor health and failing eyesight, he visited many of the scenes of the French-English conflict and tirelessly consulted archives on the subject. His magnum opus, *France and England in North America*, is a seven-part work extending from the beginning of French colonization to the conquest of New France in 1763. The first part appeared in 1865; twenty-seven years elapsed before the series was completed in 1892. His first historical work, *History of the Conspiracy of Pontiac* (1851) was not formally a part of the series. Among his other books are *The California and Oregon Trail* (1849), an account of his Western journey; *Vassall Morton* (1856), an autobiographical novel; and *The Book of Roses* (1866). This last, a book on horticulture, reflected the fact that he had been a professor of horticulture at Harvard's agricultural school (1871–72) and had originated several varieties of flowers. He also contributed historical writings to the *North American Review*, the *Atlantic Monthly*, and the *Nation*. In 1890 he published a pamphlet appealing for the wide establishment of common schools.

EDGAR ALLAN POE, poet, critic, and short-story writer, was born in Boston, Mass., January 19, 1809, and died in Baltimore, Md., October 7, 1849. He was reared in the home of his god-father, John Allan, at Richmond, Va. At the age of six Poe was placed in a school in suburban London for six years. He returned to the United States in 1821 and entered the University of Virginia when he was 17 years old. When he was forced to withdraw from the school because of gambling debts, he ran away to Boston. There he pub-lished his first volume, *Tamerlane and Other Poems* (1827). He enlisted in the Army and, through Mr. Allan's influ-ence, was admitted to West Point. Re-pelled by military discipline, he delib-erately provoked dismissal. At that point, he decided on a literary career. In 1833 his *MS Found in a Bottle* was judged the best short story in a literary competition. He moved to Richmond to write exclusively for the *Southern Literary Messenger,* where his weird tales and biting critiques won him rec-ognition. In 1836 he married his cousin, Virginia Clemm, who inspired some of his purest poetry, including *Eleonora, Annabel Lee,* and *Lenore. The Raven* stemmed from his forebodings about her desperate illness, and his grief at her death in 1847 shaped *Ulalume* and *To One in Paradise.* Indulgence in opium and intoxicants aggravated his restlessness, and he moved from one position to another. Much of his best writing, including *The Murders in the Rue Morgue, A Descent into the Mael-strom,* and *The Mystery of Marie Roget,* appeared first in *Graham's Mag-azine* in Philadelphia. In October, 1849, he fell ill in Richmond as he was start-ing for New York. Found wandering in Baltimore in a delirium, he was taken to a hospital, where he died.

A poem deserves its title only inasmuch as it excites by elevating the soul.

Edgar Allan Poe

[ELECTED IN 1910 BY 69 VOTES]

BUST by Daniel Chester French; unveiled May 20, 1922; gift of J. Sanford Saltus; unveiled by the donor; address and poem, *Israfel,* by Edwin Markham.

I would write something that would make this whole nation feel what a cursed thing slavery is.

Harriet Beecher Stowe

[ELECTED IN 1910 BY 74 VOTES]

BUST by Brenda Putnam; unveiled May 21, 1925; gift of The New York City Colony of the National Society of New England Women; unveiled by Dr. Freeman Allen, grandson of Mrs. Stowe; address by Rev. S. Parkes Cadman, D.D., President of the Federal Council of Churches of Christ in America.

HARRIET BEECHER STOWE, writer, was born in Litchfield, Conn., June 14, 1811, and died in Hartford, Conn., July 1, 1896. She was educated at and later taught in her sister Catherine's school in Hartford. In 1832 she moved to Cincinnati, where her father had been appointed a theological seminary president. She married the Reverend Calvin E. Stowe, a teacher at the seminary, and in 1850 moved to Brunswick, Me., where he had been appointed a professor at Bowdoin College. Later, he accepted a similar post at Andover, Mass. In 1843 Mrs. Stowe published *The Mayflower*, sketches about descendants of the Pilgrims. In 1851–52 the *National Era*, an anti-slavery newspaper in Washington, published serially *Uncle Tom's Cabin; or Life Among the Lowly*, Mrs. Stowe's bitter attack on slavery. She had come to know its evils during 18 years in Cincinnati, separated from Kentucky only by the Ohio River. In 1852 *Uncle Tom's Cabin* was published as a book. Within five years it had sold half a million copies in the United States alone. The book also was in great demand in England, and eventually was translated into at least 23 languages and published in innumerable editions. England lionized the author in 1853 during the European trip that provided material for her *Sunny Memories of Foreign Lands,* published the following year. None of her other works, of course, enjoyed the popularity or had the impact of *Uncle Tom's Cabin.* Another novel is *The Minister's Wooing* (1859). The *Atlantic Monthly* and other periodicals published her writings, most of which had strong sociological overtones. Mrs. Stowe also wrote a small volume of religious poems. Her husband died in 1886, and thereafter she lived in virtual seclusion in Hartford.

HENRY DAVID THOREAU, essayist and naturalist, was born in Concord, Mass., July 12, 1817, and died there May 6, 1862. Graduated from Harvard in 1837, Thoreau joined his brother in conducting a private school in Concord until 1841, when he went to live at Emerson's home, thus beginning a long friendship with Emerson and a close association with the transcendentalists. After a year in Staten Island, N.Y., (his longest residence outside Concord) Thoreau built a cabin on Emerson's land at Walden Pond in 1845. He lived there for 26 months, practicing the simple life amid the natural surroundings he loved, meditating, and writing. In 1847 he returned to his father's house with the draft of his first book, *A Week on the Concord and Merrimack Rivers,* a series of comments on life and literature. Published at his own risk in 1849, the book sold only 200 of the 1,000 copies printed. In 1853 he filled his journals with antislavery denunciations, later incorporated into *Walden,* which was published August 9, 1854. Except for a period after the Harpers Ferry raid, during which he became the first American to defend John Brown publicly, Thoreau lived quietly, working on his Concord herbarium, his weather records, and his ethnological studies of the Indian. In November, 1860, he caught a cold which developed into tuberculosis. He went to Minnesota in search of health but returned to Concord weaker than ever. Except for the two books and a few magazine articles published during his life, Thoreau's writings were edited and published posthumously. The Riverside Edition of his works (1894) in eleven volumes was superseded by the Walden Edition (1906) in twenty volumes. His poetry was published as *Poems of Nature* (1895).

Henry David Thoreau

[ELECTED IN 1960 BY 83 VOTES]

[BUST has not yet been unveiled.]

41

In this broad earth of ours,
Amid the measureless grossness and the
slag,
Enclosed and safe within its central heart,
Nestles the seed Perfection.

Walt Whitman

[ELECTED IN 1930 BY 64 VOTES]

BUST by Chester Beach; unveiled May 14, 1931; gift of *The Brooklyn Daily Eagle,* Mr. and Mrs. Harrison S. Morris, the Walt Whitman Memorial Association of Brooklyn, and other admirers of the poet; presented by Cleveland Rodgers, Associate Editor of *The Eagle;* unveiled by Mrs. Horace Traubel, friend of Whitman and widow of his biographer; address by Harrison S. Morris; a poem, *Whitman Enters the Hall of Fame,* written for the occasion by Edwin Markham, was read by the poet.

WALT WHITMAN, poet, was born at West Hills, L.I., N.Y., May 31, 1819, and died at Camden, N.J., March 26, 1892. He left Brooklyn public school at 13 to become a printer's apprentice. Between 1836 and 1848 he was associated with newspapers or magazines in Long Island, Brooklyn, and New York. His contributions included sentimental stories and some competent but undistinguished verse. In 1848 he spent three months in New Orleans. After seven years of preparation, he published the first edition of *Leaves of Grass* (1855). The unconventional style and treatment led critics to write mixed reviews; but Emerson, in a letter to the author, praised it highly. During the Civil War, Whitman sought to find his brother, George, who had been reported wounded. George had recovered by the time his brother located him at Falmouth, Va. Thereafter, Whitman devoted himself to helping both Northern and Southern casualties in Washington hospitals. He donated food and writing materials, dressed wounds, and sometimes helped in surgery. During this period he supported himself by writing newspaper articles. He also drew on his wartime experiences for his prose work, *Specimen Days,* and its poetical counterpart, *Drum Taps.* After the war he accepted a job as a government clerk in Washington. Within a few weeks, Lincoln was dead. Shortly thereafter, Whitman wrote his famous elegy, *When Lilacs Last in the Dooryard Bloom'd.* Swinburne called it "the most sonorous anthem ever chanted in the church of the world." Whitman continued to work as a clerk until he was stricken by paralysis brought on by the fatigue of his wartime volunteer work. He was on his way to recovery when his mother's death caused a relapse. However, he continued to write at his brother's home in Camden until his death.

JOHN GREENLEAF WHITTIER, abolitionist and poet, was born near Haverhill, Essex County, Mass., December 17, 1807, and died at Hampton Falls, N.H., September 7, 1892. Born and reared a Quaker, he adhered throughout his life to the denomination's liberal and independent tenets. As a boy he read heavily. At 15, having read a borrowed copy of Burns, he determined to become a poet. When he was 19 his first poem was published in the weekly *Newburyport Free Press,* edited by William Lloyd Garrison, the future emancipationist. Garrison published more of Whittier's poems and introduced his works to other editors. Thus began an association between the two men that continued for nearly four decades. At Haverhill Academy, Whittier won some recognition for his student verse. After a journalistic career in Boston and Hartford, Conn., he moved to Amesbury, Mass., in 1836, and lived there for the remainder of his life. His first book, containing both prose and verse, was *Legends of New England,* published in 1831. From then on he concentrated on verse. One of his most significant poems was dedicated to Garrison; it was read at the Philadelphia convention at which the Anti-Slavery Society was formed in 1833. Whittier, a prominent delegate at that founding session, reached heights of eloquence on behalf of emancipation. The same year he issued a pamphlet, *Justice and Expediency,* that provoked heated discussion in both the North and the South on the slavery question. Having become an active Whig, he was sent to the Massachusetts Legislature in 1835. He was closely associated with the *Atlantic Monthly* from its founding in 1857. It was the appearance of *Snowbound* in 1866 that brought him national acclaim and financial reward. His unsophisticated verse has an appealing ballad-like quality.

Making his rustic reed of song
A weapon in the war with wrong,
Yoking his fancy to the breaking plough
That beam-deep turned the soil
For Truth to spring and grow.

John Greenleaf Whittier

[ELECTED IN 1905 BY 53 VOTES]

BUST by Rudulph Evans; unveiled May 10, 1928; gift of the American Members of the Society of Friends; presented by President David M. Edwards of Earlham College, Richmond, Indiana; unveiled by James Weldon Johnson, former U.S. Consul in Nicaragua and Venezuela; address by Hon. Henry van Dyke, former American Minister to The Hague. A poem on Whittier, by Edwin Markham, was also read.

The South Gate of the Colonnade.

II

EDUCATORS

MARK HOPKINS, educator and theologian, was born at Stockbridge, Mass., February 4, 1802, and died at Williamstown, Mass., June 17, 1887. After graduation from Williams in 1824 he studied medicine but interrupted his studies for two years to tutor at Williams. Finally, in 1829, he received his M.D. degree from Berkshire Medical College at Pittsfield, Mass. For a few months he practiced medicine in New York City and in Binghamton, N.Y. At that point, he was called back to Williams, this time as a professor in rhetoric and moral philosophy. Six years later he was named president of Williams, a post he held for 36 years. He was married on Christmas Day, 1832. He and his wife, Mary, had ten children. During his early years at Williams the college lacked adequate library materials, a fact sometimes cited as the reason for Hopkins having developed a teaching system which did not require elaborate textbooks. He used dialogue and the personal approach so successfully that President James A. Garfield once remarked that the ideal college would be one in which Hopkins sat on one end of a log and the student on the other. Hopkins believed that moral philosophy was a subject which had an innate, direct appeal for the mind of the learner. He based his philosophy on his belief that God is a rational being and that whatever is created by the rational—specifically man and nature—must also be rational. Although Hopkins had never attended a theological school, he was licensed (1833) to preach by the Berkshire Association of Congregational Ministers; three years later, he was ordained. He delivered many sermons, but his enduring fame rests upon his skill as a teacher. He also lectured before many scientific and literary societies. His writings included *Evidences of Christianity* and *The Law of Love, and Love as a Law.*

What higher conception of virtue can we have than that at every point of a man's life his conscience should demand and he should render that love which is the fulfilling of the law.

Mark Hopkins

[ELECTED IN 1915 BY 69 VOTES]

BUST by Hans Hoerbst; replica unveiled May 20, 1922; gift of Williams College Alumni; unveiled, with address, by President Harry A. Garfield of Williams College.

There is nothing in the Universe that I fear but that I shall not know all my duty, or fail to do it.

Mary Lyon

[ELECTED IN 1905 BY 59 VOTES]

BUST by Laura Gardin Fraser; unveiled May 5, 1927; gift of the Mount Holyoke College Alumnae Association; presented by Mrs. Walter E. Schuster, President of the Association; unveiled by Miss Lucy Street, Chairman of Mount Holyoke College Community; address by Dr. Mary E. Woolley, President of Mount Holyoke.

MARY LYON, educator, was born in Buckland, Mass., February 28, 1797, and died in South Hadley, Mass., March 5, 1849. A pioneer in higher education for women, she started teaching at the age of 18. With money earned from spinning and weaving she attended Sanderson Academy at Ashfield, Mass., where she displayed quick-wittedness and a passion for learning. Later, she was appointed a teacher and associate principal at Sanderson and, in 1824, became a teacher at the Adams Female Academy at Londonderry, N.H. Four years later she and the Adams principal founded a seminary at Ipswich, Mass. In 1834 Miss Lyon resigned to devote herself to founding a girls' seminary which would combine high academic principles and low cost. Despite indifference and antagonism in some influential quarters, she raised funds to open, on November 8, 1837, a school at South Hadley under the name of Mount Holyoke Female Seminary (now Mount Holyoke College). There were about 80 pupils in the initial enrollment, but in the second year 400 applicants had to be turned away for lack of space. The regular instructors were women, supplemented by lecturers from the Williams and Amherst faculties. To help keep costs low, a specific household task was assigned to each student. The original curriculum included mathematics, English, science, philosophy, and Latin, with the promise that music and modern languages would be added as soon as feasible. On a salary of $200 a year, Miss Lyon worked tirelessly, enlarging and improving the school until it had gained a national reputation for its enlightened curriculum and high academic standards. She remained president until her death. Among her writings are *Tendencies of the Principles Embraced and the System Adopted in the Mount Holyoke Female Seminary* (1840) and the *Missionary Offering* (1843).

HORACE MANN, educator, was born at Franklin, Mass., May 4, 1796, and died at Yellow Springs, Ohio, August 2, 1859. The once enlightened public school system was in chaos during his childhood. Until he was 16 he had never attended school for more than ten weeks in any one year. Then, aided by a brilliant itinerant tutor named Barrett, he prepared himself in six months for the Sophomore class at Brown University. He was graduated with honors in 1819, entered law school, and was admitted to the bar in 1823. He practiced law for 14 years and served in both houses of the Massachusetts Legislature. He was Senate president from 1835 until he was appointed the first secretary of the new State Board of Education in 1837. In that capacity he achieved sweeping reforms in the public school system: higher pay for teachers, a minimum school year of six months, a $2,000,000 appropriation for new buildings, and the establishment of 50 new high schools. He was also instrumental in establishing three state normal schools—the first in the nation. While he had little authority, he persuaded community leaders to support his educational program. Many of his ideas spread to other states through his 12 annual reports to the Board of Education, reports which contained both analyses of problems and accounts of progress. Twice he met and overcame opposition. On one occasion he prevailed against groups that demanded the teaching of sectarian religion in public schools. On the other he conquered criticism caused by his praise of German educational methods. In 1848 he resigned to serve in the United States House of Representatives. Four years later he was defeated as the Free Soil party's candidate for Massachusetts governor. He spent his last years as president of Antioch College at Yellow Springs, Ohio.

The Common School is the greatest discovery ever made by man. It is supereminent in its universality and in the timeliness of the aid it proffers. . . . The Common School can train up children in the elements of all good knowledge and of virtue.

Horace Mann

[ELECTED IN 1900 BY 67 VOTES]

Bust by Adolph A. Weinman; unveiled May 8, 1930; gift of the Horace Mann School of New York and the Horace Mann League; unveiled by Horace Mann, grandson of the educator, and by his daughter Katharine; address by Hon. William John Cooper, U.S. Commissioner of Education. This bust replaced a former one, the replica of a work by an unknown sculptor; unveiled May 30, 1907; gift for the teachers of New York, by the National Education Association.

The smallest village, the plainest home, give ample space for the resources of the college-trained woman.

Alice Freeman Palmer

[ELECTED IN 1920 BY 53 VOTES]

BUST by Evelyn Longman; unveiled May 13, 1924; gift of Wellesley College; unveiled by Professor George H. Palmer, husband of Alice Freeman Palmer; address by Dr. James Rowland Angell, President of Yale University.

ALICE FREEMAN PALMER, educator, was born in Colesville, N.Y., February 21, 1855, and died in Paris, December 6, 1902. Her mother was a woman of intelligence and courage—attributes displayed early in life by Alice. At three, she taught herself to read and at four entered school. In 1865 she enrolled at nearby Windsor Academy, a coeducational preparatory school. She was only 14 when she became engaged to a young Windsor teacher; a year later she dissolved the engagement to concentrate on obtaining a college education. Overcoming parental reluctance, Alice took the University of Michigan entrance examination at 17 and failed. However, her personality so impressed the university's president that he prevailed on the examiners to admit her on probation. Her studies were interrupted by ill health and financial difficulties, but she finally graduated in 1876 and taught in Lake Geneva, Wis., and in Saginaw, Mich. Twice in that period she declined offers to teach at Wellesley. In 1879 she accepted the third invitation and thus, at 24, became head of Wellesley's history department. Two years later she was appointed vice-president and acting president, and in 1882 she became president. In the six years of her administration she reorganized and strengthened the curriculum and faculty. She also helped found the Association of Collegiate Alumnae (forerunner of the American Association of University Women), and in 1884 was a delegate at the International Conference on Education in London. Three years later she married George Herbert Palmer, a Harvard philosophy professor. From 1892 to 1895 she was dean of women at the University of Chicago. Although she had resigned the Wellesley presidency, she maintained strong school ties. At the time of her death during a visit to Europe, she was a Wellesley trustee.

BOOKER T. WASHINGTON, educator, was born in Franklin County near Hale's Ford, Va., about April 5, 1858, and died at Tuskegee Institute, Alabama, November 14, 1915. After the Civil War he worked in salt furnaces and coal mines in Malden, W.Va. As a janitor he then worked his way through Hampton Agricultural and Industrial School; he was graduated with honors in 1875. He taught school at Malden and later studied at Wayland Seminary in Washington, D.C. In 1879 he was appointed an instructor at Hampton, where he had the responsibility of training 75 Indians. In 1881 with the aid of General Samuel Chapman Armstrong, the principal of Hampton, Washington set out to organize a school at Tuskegee, Ala. Recognizing the importance of industrial and agricultural training for the American Negro, he, as head of Tuskegee Institute, emphasized these skills in the curriculum. An accomplished speaker, he went on extended lecture tours through the United States and Europe to raise funds for Tuskegee. He expanded and developed the institute and in 1900 founded the National Negro Business League, an organization dedicated to the task of making its members better citizens of their respective communities. His work as an educator earned him national and international recognition. He received honorary degrees from Dartmouth and Harvard. In 1901 he wrote his autobiography, *Up From Slavery*. In addition, he edited *Tuskegee and Its People* (1905), and was the author of several other books, among them *The Future of the American Negro* (1899), *Life of Frederick Douglass* (1907), *The Story of the Negro* (1909), and *My Larger Education* (1911). He died the day after returning from a trip to New York, where he had collapsed from overwork.

The highest test of the civilization of a race is its willingness to extend a helping hand to the less fortunate.

Booker T. Washington

[ELECTED IN 1945 BY 57 VOTES]

BUST by Richmond Barthé; unveiled May 23, 1946, gift of Hampton and Tuskegee Institutes, The Foster Hall Collection of the University of Pittsburgh, and Mr. Stephen J. Wigmore; formal presentation by Dr. Frederick D. Patterson, President of Tuskegee Institute; unveiled by Miss Gloria D. Washington, granddaughter of Washington; tribute to Washington by Dr. Jackson Davis of the General Education Board; another address by Dr. Ralph P. Bridgman, President of Hampton Institute. The cloth which unveiled the bronze was formally presented by the Director of the Hall of Fame, Dr. James Rowland Angell, to Mrs. Portia Washington Pittman, daughter of the educator. The Hampton Institute Creative Dance Group presented a dramatic pantomime interpreting the life of Booker T. Washington. Music by Dorothy Maynor and The Tuskegee Choir.

Reason and religion teach that we too are primary existences, that it is for us to move in the orbit of our duty around the holy center of perfection, the companions not the satellites of men.

Emma Willard

[ELECTED IN 1905 BY 50 VOTES]

BUST by Frances Grimes; unveiled May 9, 1929; gift of the alumnae of the Emma Willard School, Mrs. Crawford R. Green, Chairman of the Committee; unveiled by Miss Emma Willard Keyes, great-great-granddaughter of Mrs. Willard; address by Miss Eliza Kellas, Principal of the Emma Willard School, Troy, N.Y.

EMMA WILLARD, educator, was born in Berlin, Conn., February 23, 1787, and died in Troy, N.Y., April 15, 1870. She began teaching at the age of 16, and by 1807 had become principal of a girls' academy at Middlebury, Vt. Married to Dr. John Willard in 1809, she opened her Middlebury home in 1814 as a girls' boarding school. Here she introduced improved teaching methods and an expanded curriculum previously unknown in girls' schools. In 1819 she addressed to the New York Legislature a treatise titled "A Plan for Improving Female Education." The plea for state aid in founding girls' schools and for equality of educational opportunity for women won Governor DeWitt Clinton's support even though the majority of the legislators ridiculed the idea. Later that year a seminary for girls was established in Waterford, N.Y. In 1823 Mrs. Willard moved the school to Troy, N.Y., where city officials presented her with a building for the institution, thereafter known as the Troy Female Seminary. In 1838, some 13 years after her husband's death, she relinquished her school duties to her son and married Dr. Christopher C. Yates. They were divorced in 1843. During her travels in Europe in 1830, she helped found a girls' school in Athens and gathered material for her book, *Journal and Letters from France and Great Britain* (1833). Proceeds from the sale of the book went to the Troy seminary. Between 1845 and 1847 she traveled 8,000 miles through the West and South, spreading the gospel of education for women. Her schoolbooks were used widely and translated into European and Asiatic languages. The subjects dealt with in the books included geography, American history, physiology, and astronomy. She also wrote verse, including the widely known poem, *Rocked in the Cradle of the Deep.*

III

PREACHERS, THEOLOGIANS

HENRY WARD BEECHER, clergyman, was born in Litchfield, Conn., June 24, 1813, and died in Brooklyn, N.Y., March 8, 1887. After graduation from Amherst in 1834 he entered Lane Theological Seminary in Cincinnati. In the period following, he preached in Ohio and Indiana churches, was ordained in 1838 by the New School Presbytery of Cincinnati, and, in 1847, became pastor of the Plymouth Congregational Church in Brooklyn. His fiery personality attracted people to his church in increasing numbers. A man of inexhaustible energy, he was an imposing figure in the pulpit with his long hair cascading down to his collar. When his church burned down, it had to be replaced by a much larger one to accommodate the estimated 2,500 who attended his sermons each week. A passionate speaker on current issues, he thought slavery was evil but believed that if no new slave states were admitted to the Union, slavery would be confined to the South and eventually would die out of its own accord. Nevertheless, he sanctioned the sheltering of runaway slaves in defiance of the Fugitive Slave Law. In 1874 he was sued for $100,000 by the husband of a woman with whom Beecher was charged with improper conduct. A hung jury (9 to 3 in Beecher's favor) acquitted him, and 18 months later a council of Congregational churches declared that no proof of his misconduct existed. A man of great charm and tact, Beecher cheerfully entered into community activities such as house-building or firefighting. In 1844 he published his sermons under the title *Seven Lectures to Young Men.* He was editor of *The Christian Union* in 1870–71 and at his death was engaged in writing *Life of Jesus the Christ,* which was finished later by his sons. When Beecher died, some 40,000 mourners attended his casket at the church.

It matters little to me what school of theology rises or falls, so only that Christ may rise in all his Father's glory, full-orbed upon the darkness of this world.

Henry Ward Beecher

[ELECTED IN 1900 BY 64 VOTES]

BUST by Massey Rhind; unveiled May 22, 1923; gift of William A. Nash; unveiled by Colonel William C. Beecher, son of the former pastor of Plymouth Church; address by the Rev. Newell Dwight Hillis, of Plymouth Church.

If you limit the search for truth and forbid men anywhere, in any way, to seek knowledge, you paralyze the vital force of truth itself.

Phillips Brooks

[ELECTED IN 1910 BY 60 VOTES]

BUST by Daniel Chester French; unveiled May 13, 1924; gift of Trinity Church, Boston; unveiled by Miss Josephine Brooks, niece of Bishop Brooks; address by the Rev. Leighton Parks, D.D.

PHILLIPS BROOKS, clergyman, was born in Boston, Mass., December 13, 1835, and died there January 23, 1893. A member of the family which founded Phillips Exeter Academy, Phillips Andover Academy, and Andover Theological Seminary, he was the second of six sons, four of whom entered the ministry. After graduating from Harvard and the theological seminary at Alexandria, Va., he was ordained a deacon in 1859 and began his ministry in Philadelphia. In 1862, as rector of Holy Trinity Church in Philadelphia, he attracted wide attention with a sermon titled "Character, Life and Death of Mr. Lincoln," preached while Lincoln's body lay in state in Independence Hall. He wrote the words to *O Little Town of Bethlehem* for his Sunday school class; it was first sung at Christmas in 1868. Brooks was unrivaled in the pulpit as an orator. He held a strong belief that "preaching is the communication of truth by man to man" and that, therefore, a minister must understand and live what he considers to be the truth. In 1869 he became rector of Boston's Trinity Church, the stronghold of Episcopalianism. In 1880 he delivered the Bohlen Lectures in Philadelphia, accepted an invitation to preach in Westminster Abbey, and became the first American to preach before the Queen in the Royal Chapel at Windsor. He was elected bishop in 1891 on the first ballot of the diocesan convention. He held that office for 15 months, until his death. Boston held memorial services in his honor, and $95,000 was raised from spontaneous contributions for a bronze statue which today stands near Trinity Church. The Phillips Brooks House at Harvard also was established in his honor. He is also memorialized in a stained glass window at St. Margaret's, the parish church of Westminster in the Abbey's shadow in London.

WILLIAM ELLERY CHANNING, clergyman, was born in Newport, R.I., April 7, 1780, and died in Bennington, Vt., October 2, 1842. Channing, known as the leader of the Unitarian movement in the United States, began his career after graduation from Harvard by tutoring for 18 months in Richmond, Va. Overwork during these months left him a semi-invalid for the rest of his life. In 1802 he was appointed to a Harvard proctorial office that left him leisure time for the pursuit of his own studies. In 1803 he was ordained and installed as a minister of the Federal Street Church in Boston, a pastorate that he held until his death. He married his cousin, Ruth Gibbs, in 1814. The following year theological differences in the New England Congregational churches became acute. After lengthy deliberation he decided to become leader of the new Unitarian movement. In 1819 he preached a sermon defending Unitarian rights to Christian fellowship, and in 1820 he organized the Berry Street Conference of liberal ministers, from which grew the American Unitarian Association. He rejected the Calvinist idea that humans by nature are depraved and incapable of goodness. He put forth his beliefs in a sermon, "The Moral Argument Against Calvinism." "Channing Unitarianism" came to stand for religious liberalism and influenced Bryant, Longfellow, Emerson, Lowell, and Holmes. Channing was an early advocate of adult education and suggested that funds raised through the sale of public lands be used for public education. He also was an advocate of temperance— not by legislative means but by "increasing the innocent gratifications in a community." Additionally, Channing was an ardent Abolitionist and an outspoken critic of the War of 1812. The Massachusetts Peace Society was organized in his study.

I think of God as the Father and Inspirer of the Soul—of Christ as its Redeemer and model; of Christianity as given to enlighten, perfect, and glorify it.

William Ellery Channing

[ELECTED IN 1900 BY 58 VOTES]

BUST by Herbert Adams; unveiled May 5, 1927; gift of the American Unitarian Association; presented by Rev. Samuel A. Eliot, President of the Association; unveiled by Mrs. William Rotch Wister, granddaughter of Channing; address by Rev. Francis G. Peabody, D.D., of Harvard University.

God is the head of the universal system of existence, from whom all is perfectly derived and on whom all is most absolutely dependent, whose Being and Beauty is the sum and comprehension of all existence and excellence.

Jonathan Edwards

[ELECTED IN 1900 BY 82 VOTES]

BUST by Charles Grafly; unveiled May 12, 1926; gift of the Presbyterian Church of the United States of America; unveiled by Dr. Marion Edwards Park, President of Bryn Mawr College and a great-great-granddaughter of Edwards; address by Rev. Charles R. Erdman, D.D., Moderator of the Presbyterian Church.

JONATHAN EDWARDS, theologian, was born at East Windsor, Conn., October 5, 1703, and died at Princeton, N.J., March 22, 1758. Reared in an environment of Puritan piety and intellectual vigor, he entered Yale at 13 and was graduated as valedictorian before he was 17. After two years of study for the ministry, he accepted for a brief time a New York pastorate. He received his M.A. from Yale in 1723. In 1727 he joined Solomon Stoddard, his grandfather, who was pastor at Northampton, Mass. In the same year he married Sarah Pierrepont. Influenced by his studies of Newton, the Cambridge Platonists, and especially Locke's *Essay on the Human Understanding*, he outlined in a series of notes his philosophical theology, stating the doctrines of Calvinism in terms of contemporary philosophy. When Stoddard died in 1729, Edwards became sole pastor at Northampton, the largest and wealthiest Massachusetts congregation outside of Boston. His first published sermon, which explored New England's moral decay, was preached to the Boston clergy in 1731. It was a declaration of a fundamental article of his creed: God's absolute sovereignty in the work of salvation. Thus he was a leader in the "Great Awakening," the religious revival that swept the colonies a decade later. However, Edward's relations with his congregation deteriorated. Climaxing a controversy over qualifications for communion, he was dismissed in 1750. The following year he became pastor of the frontier church at Stockbridge, Mass., where he wrote his famous work on the *Freedom of the Will* (1754), assailing the idea of a self-determining will. In 1757 he became president of the college at Princeton (later Princeton University). A short time later he contracted smallpox from an inoculation and died.

ROGER WILLIAMS, clergyman, was born in London, probably in 1603, and died in Providence, R.I., about March, 1683. He was a protégé of Sir Edward Coke, the eminent English jurist, who obtained a Charterhouse School scholarship for him in 1621. Later, Williams won honors at Pembroke College, Cambridge, where he prepared himself for the ministry. He married Mary Barnard, and together they sailed for Massachusetts in 1630. Here, because of his tolerant views, he ran afoul of the Puritan authorities. At Salem, he declared that civil governments had no power to enforce their ecclesiastic views, and he assailed the oath of obedience demanded of colonists. He was found guilty of preaching "newe & dangerous opinions" and was banished from the colony. When the authorities learned that Williams and his followers planned to colonize in Narragansett, they tried to arrest him; but he escaped in midwinter and was sheltered by Indians. By 1636 he had succeeded in founding the Rhode Island settlement at Providence. Several years later the Puritans, negotiating for an autonomous New England Confederation, decided to seek a Narragansett patent from London in order to curb what they considered to be the dangerous political and religious liberalism practiced in the Williams settlement. However, Williams outmaneuvered them by getting to London first and there using his considerable influence to obtain a patent for the entire Narragansett area. An active pamphleteer for democratic principles, he also was a champion of Indian rights. Twice, however, he reluctantly sided with the Puritans against the Indians—once in the Pequot War and again in the King Philip's War. He lived to see Providence and Warwick reduced to ashes in Indian warfare, and the Narragansett tribe that he had championed decimated and enslaved.

To proclaim a true and absolute soul freedom to all the people of the land impartially so that no person be forced to pray, nor pray otherwise than as his soul believeth and consenteth.

Roger Williams

[ELECTED IN 1920 BY 66 VOTES]

BUST by Hermon A. MacNeil; unveiled May 12, 1926; gift of The Rhode Island Society of the Colonial Dames; unveiled by Mrs. John D. Rockefeller, Jr., descendant in three lines from Williams; address by Rabbi Stephen S. Wise.

A portion of the Colonnade. The bust of
Susan B. Anthony is in the foreground.

IV

HUMANITARIANS

SOCIAL AND ECONOMIC REFORMERS

SUSAN B. ANTHONY, reformer and suffragette, was born at Adams, Mass., February 15, 1820, and died at Rochester, N.Y., March 13, 1906. A member of a large Quaker family, she received her early education from her father, who conducted a school in their home. She later attended Deborah Moulson's Boarding School near Philadelphia in preparation for a teaching career. After many years of teaching, sometimes for $1.50 a week (then considered good money for a woman), she gave up her career (1850) and devoted herself to the problems of the day. She became interested in temperance and organized the Woman's State Temperance Society of New York. In 1869 she became chairman of the executive committee of the National Woman Suffrage Association. She lost some support during this postwar period by insisting that the vote be withheld from freedmen until it was also given to women. The remainder of her life was dedicated to this cause; and in 1892 she was elected president of the National Woman Suffrage Association, a post she held until retirement at 80. It was not until 14 years after her death that the Nineteenth Amendment, giving women the right to vote, was enacted; but to her must go the credit for pointing the way for other women who took up her work. In one of her most spectacular actions, she led a group of women to the polls in Rochester, N.Y. (1872) to test the right of women to the franchise under the terms of the Fourteenth Amendment. Her arrest, trial, and sentence to a fine (which she refused to pay) were a *cause célèbre*. Other women followed her example until finally the case was decided against them by the United States Supreme Court. Her power lay in her intelligence, her strong personality, and her remarkable singleness of purpose.

The day will come when man will recognize woman as his peer, not only at the fireside but in the councils of the nation. Then . . . will there be the perfect comradeship . . . between the sexes that shall result in the highest development of the race. . . .

Susan B. Anthony

[ELECTED IN 1950 BY 72 VOTES]

BUST by Brenda Putnam; unveiled May 18, 1952; gift of The National Federation of Business and Professional Women's Clubs, Inc. In addition to the principal fund provided by the Federation, a contribution was received from The General Alliance of Unitarian and Other Liberal Christian Women. Formal presentation by Hon. Sarah T. Hughes, Judge of the Fourteenth District Court, Dallas, Texas, and President, The National Federation of Business and Professional Women's Clubs, Inc.; unveiled by Mrs. Ann Anthony Bacon, niece of Susan B. Anthony. Address by Hon. Florence Ellinwood Allen, Judge of the United States Court of Appeals for the Sixth Circuit. Music for the ceremony by Miss Gladys Swarthout and the New York University Chapel Choir.

Were I asked to define in a sentence the thought and purpose of the Woman's Christian Temperance Union, I should reply it is to make the whole world homelike.

Frances Elizabeth Willard

[ELECTED IN 1910 BY 55 VOTES]

BUST by Lorado Taft; unveiled May 22, 1923; gift of the National Woman's Christian Temperance Union; unveiled by O. H. Willard, kinsman of Miss Willard; address by Miss Anna A. Gordon, President N.W.C.T.U.

FRANCES ELIZABETH WILLARD, reformer, was born in Churchville, N.Y., September 28, 1839, and died in New York City, February 18, 1898. During her childhood the family moved westward, first to Ohio and then to the Wisconsin wilderness. Life was lonely until the girl went to college at 17, first to the Milwaukee Female College and then to the Northwestern Female College in Evanston, Ill. After a romance ended in a broken engagement, she began teaching in country schools near Evanston, at Pittsburgh Female College, and at Genesee Wesleyan Seminary at Lima, N.Y. During 1871–74 she was president of the Evanston College for Ladies. She was scarcely out of her teens before she started writing articles, and her first book was published when she was only 25. In 1868 she sailed for Europe and for two years toured the Continent. Upon returning, she lectured on her travels, thereby beginning her public speaking career. In 1874 she found her life work in the temperance movement which was sweeping the country. She became president of the Chicago Woman's Temperance Union and from that office rose in 1879 to the presidency of the National Woman's Temperance Union and, in 1891, to the presidency of the World's Woman's Christian Temperance Union. She helped to organize the Prohibition party in 1882. She also was president of the National Council of Women for some years, but her main concern was with temperance. As head of its organizations, she toured the United States in 1883, speaking in every state and territory. She wrote lectures, books, and slogans, and regarded the cause as worth any amount of personal sacrifice. Her published works included *Women and Temperance, A Classic Town; The Story of Evanston,* and *How I Learned to Ride the Bicycle.*

V

SCIENTISTS

LOUIS AGASSIZ, naturalist, was born at Motier, Switzerland, May 28, 1807, and died at Cambridge, Mass., December 14, 1873. He was educated at the Zurich medical school, at Heidelberg, and at the Munich university, from which he received an M.D. degree in 1830. He was a distinguished scientist even before coming to the United States at the age of 39. While in Paris he studied under Cuvier and was a friend of Humboldt's. He made several pioneering contributions to the study of fishes, fossils, and glaciers. His first published work, which appeared when he was 21, was *Fishes of Brazil*. It was compiled from data brought back from South America by Martius and Spix. He produced a five-volume atlas of fossil fishes, illustrated by his first wife, Cecile Braun Agassiz. His career in the United States began in 1846 when he was invited to deliver the Lowell Institute Lectures in Boston. Later, after his first wife died in Europe, he settled permanently in America, accepting the post of professor of zoology and geology at the Lawrence Scientific School of Harvard. In 1850 he married Elizabeth Cabot Cary, who later became president of Radcliffe College. She accompanied him on an expedition to Brazil and on a voyage that took them to California in the course of an Atlantic and Pacific coastline survey. Agassiz was a major force in awakening American interest in natural history. As a teacher he trained an entire generation of naturalists. He was instrumental in establishing the Harvard Museum of Comparative Zoology (frequently called the Agassiz Museum) and was its first curator. He was much sought after as a lecturer. His most famous writing is his essay on classification, found in the first volume of his four-volume *Contributions to the Natural History of the United States* (1857).

Scientific investigations should be inspired by a purpose as animating to the general sympathy as was the religious zeal which built the Cathedral of Cologne and the Basilica of St. Peter.

Louis Agassiz

[ELECTED IN 1915 BY 65 VOTES]

BUST by Anna Hyatt Huntington; unveiled May 10, 1928; gift of the American Association for the Advancement of Science and of an admirer of Agassiz; presented by Dr. J. Walter Fewkes of the Smithsonian Institution, a pupil of Agassiz; unveiled by George Agassiz, grandson of the scientist; address by Professor Henry Fairfield Osborn, President of the American Association for the Advancement of Science and President of the American Museum of Natural History, read by Dr. Robert Cushman Murphy, Curator of Oceanic Birds at the American Museum of Natural History.

The productions of nature soon became my playmates. I felt that an intimacy with them not consisting of friendship, merely, but bordering on phrenzy, must accompany my steps through life.

John James Audubon

[ELECTED IN 1900 BY 67 VOTES]

BUST by A. Stirling Calder; unveiled May 5, 1927; gift of the Group of Societies at 155th Street and Broadway [The American Geographic Society, The Museum of the American Indian, The Hispanic Society of America, The Numismatic Society, and The American Academy of Arts and Letters]; presented by Dr. George Bird Grinnell, naturalist, and trustee of the Hispanic Society; unveiled by Ernest F. Tyler, great-grandson of Audubon; address by Dr. Frank M. Chapman, Curator of the Bird Department of the American Museum of Natural History.

JOHN JAMES AUDUBON, artist and naturalist, was born in Aux Cayes, Haiti (then Les Cayes, Santo Domingo), April 26, 1785, and died in New York City, January 27, 1851. He went to France with his father, and by the time he was 15 he had begun sketching French birds. After a short term in military school, he studied drawing in Paris under David. In 1803 he left France to live on his father's estate near Philadelphia. Here he began his studies of American birds. In the first such experiment on bird migration in America, he banded some baby peewees and discovered the following year that they returned to nest in the same area. A quarrel with his father's agent sent Audubon back to France, but he soon returned. He and a partner opened a general store in Louisville, Ky., in 1807, the year before he married Lucy Bakewell. Later, the store was floated down the Ohio by flatboat and re-established in Henderson, Ky. But owing in part to Audubon's preoccupation with bird life, the business failed, forcing him to become an itinerant painter. In 1820, as a taxidermist at Cincinnati's Western Museum, he decided to publish his bird drawings. He traveled widely, sketching and paying his way by painting portraits and even street signs. His wife worked as a governess to help defray expenses. Unable to find a publisher in America, he went to Europe and was an immediate success. He was elected to the Royal Society of Edinburgh. In London, the King himself subscribed to *Birds of America*, which had begun to appear in elephant folio in London in 1827. It took 11 years to complete publication. Meanwhile, Audubon began work in Edinburgh on the text of *Birds of America*, to be called *Ornithological Biography*. Upon his return home in 1831, he was hailed as America's foremost naturalist.

JOSIAH WILLARD GIBBS, mathematical physicist, was born in New Haven, Conn., February 11, 1839, and died there April 28, 1903. He was a student at Yale College at 15 and was graduated in 1858. After receiving his doctorate in 1863 he taught Latin for two years at Yale and science for a third year. After three years in Europe, in 1871 he was appointed professor of mathematical physics at Yale where he remained until his death. From the start his writings were brilliant and informative. He continued the study of his theory of thermodynamics, the basis for the major part of modern physical chemistry and chemical engineering. In 1876 he issued the first half of his great work, *On the Equilibrium of Heterogeneous Substances,* which appeared in the Transactions of the Connecticut Academy of Arts and Sciences. The same periodical published the second half in 1878. Another paper on thermodynamics appeared under the title *Electrochemical Thermodynamics* in Report of the British Association for the Advancement of Science, in 1886. From 1882 to 1889 he devoted himself principally to the theories of optics. He set forth some of these theories in an article titled *Notes on the Electromagnetic Theory of Light* in the *American Journal of Science.* In 1902 his *Elementary Principles in Statistical Mechanics* was published in the Yale Bicentennial series. With his insatiable curiosity, Gibbs was essentially a student. He received many honorary degrees, including ones from Williams, Princeton, Erlangen, and Christiania. He was a member of the National Academy of Sciences, vice-president of the American Association for the Advancement of Science, a member of the American Philosophical Society, and a foreign honorary member or correspondent of a large number of European learned societies.

One of the principal objects of theoretical research is to find the point of view from which the subject appears in its greatest simplicity.

Josiah Willard Gibbs

[ELECTED IN 1950 BY 64 VOTES]

BUST by Stanley Martineau; unveiled December 1, 1957; gift of Yale University and The American Chemical Society, with contributions from Dr. Ralph G. Van Name, the Fisher Scientific Company, the M. W. Kellogg Company, the National Academy of Sciences, the American Philosophical Society, the American Association for the Advancement of Science, The American Academy of Arts and Sciences, and numerous friends of Gibbs; formal presentation by Dr. John G. Kirkwood, Sterling Professor of Chemistry, Director of Sciences, Yale University; unveiled by Dr. Ralph G. Van Name, Research Associate Emeritus in Chemistry, Yale University and a nephew of Professor Gibbs; address by Dr. Detlev W. Bronk, President, The National Academy of Sciences.

I confidently expect that in the future even more than in the past, faith in an order, which is the basis of science, will not be dissevered from faith in an Ordainer, which is the basis of religion.

Asa Gray

[ELECTED IN 1900 BY 51 VOTES]

BUST by Chester Beach; unveiled May 21, 1925; gift of The Gray Herbarium of Harvard University and of friends and relatives of Dr. Gray; unveiled by Miss Alice A. Gray, niece of Dr. Gray; tribute, by phonofilm, by Dr. Charles W. Eliot, President Emeritus of Harvard, and address by Professor Benjamin L. Robinson, Curator of the Herbarium.

ASA GRAY, botanist, was born in Paris, N.Y., November 18, 1810, and died in Cambridge, Mass., January 30, 1888. As a youth (1827), he read an encyclopedia article on botany, and from then on it was his predominant interest. Although he received an M.D. degree, he never practiced medicine but devoted the following decade to field trips and lectures on botany. His first book, issued in 1834, was illustrated with dried specimens and received high praise for being both beautiful and scientifically useful. He became curator of the New York Lyceum of Natural History and collaborated with Dr. John Torrey on *Flora of North America*. He accepted a botany professorship at the University of Michigan and sailed for Europe in 1834 to buy books for the school, then in the process of being organized. Later, after field trips in Virginia and North Carolina, he published the *Botanical Text-Book* (1842), which became a model in the field because of its standardization of technical terms. Gray accepted a natural history professorship at Harvard and in 1848 married Jane Lathrop Loring. Their house in the Harvard Botanical Garden became a social center for botanists from the United States and Europe. He was a founder of the National Academy of Science and president of many scientific organizations. For half a century he contributed to the *American Journal of Science*. His descriptive monograph on the botany of Japan attracted wide attention. In all, he was the author or coauthor of some 350 textbooks, monographs, descriptive studies, and papers, and was considered a pioneer in the field of plant geography. Scientists sought his advice on classifying specimens collected by expeditions throughout the world. He was the chief American advocate of Darwin after the English naturalist had explained his natural selection theories to Gray in 1857.

JOSEPH HENRY, physicist, was born in Albany, N.Y., December 17, 1797, and died in Washington, D.C., May 13, 1878. He studied at Albany Academy with the intention of preparing for medicine but turned instead to physics. In 1826 he was elected a professor of mathematics and natural philosophy at Albany Academy and began experiments with electromagnets. In one famous demonstration, he wound silk from his wife's wedding dress around a wire for insulation, spiraled it repeatedly in many layers around an iron core, and produced an electromagnet infinitely more powerful than the electromagnets of the day. His technique was immediately adopted universally and is used to this day. In 1831 he constructed the first model of an electric telegraph with audible signal by winding a mile of wire around his classroom and attaching a bell which rang when an electrical impulse reached it. Henry also detected the inducted current independently of Faraday—and possibly before his English colleague; the principle opened the way for an age of electric-powered machinery. Henry was given credit, however, for discovering the principle of self-induction; the unit of inductance is called the "henry" in recognition of that fact. In 1832 he was elected professor of natural philosophy at the College of New Jersey, now Princeton. During his years there he made several important discoveries, among them the electric relay, the principle of the transformer, and developments in the field of radio telegraphy. Many of his findings were not published until other inventors had beaten him into print. In 1846, he left Princeton to become the first secretary of the Smithsonian Institution. He was president of the National Academy of Sciences from 1868 until his death. His collected works were published posthumously.

I may say I was the first to bring the electro magnet into the condition necessary to its use in telegraphy and also to point out its application to the telegraph.

Joseph Henry

[ELECTED IN 1915 BY 56 VOTES]

BUST by John Flanagan; unveiled May 13, 1924; gift of the American Institute of Electrical Engineers; unveiled by Thomas Alva Edison; address by Frank B. Jewett, Past-President of the Institute.

Pathfinder of the Seas.

Matthew Fontaine Maury

[ELECTED IN 1930 BY 66 VOTES]

BUST by F. William Sievers; unveiled May 14, 1931; gift of the United Daughters of the Confederacy; presented by Mrs. L. M. Bashinsky, President of the U.D.C.; unveiled by Matthew Fontaine Maury, 3rd, great-grandson of Maury; addresses by Professor S. A. Mitchell, Director of Leander McCormick Observatory, University of Virginia, and Rear-Admiral Walter R. Gherardi, U.S.N., Hydrographer of the Bureau of Navigation, and a letter on Maury's interest in Antarctic exploration from Rear-Admiral Richard E. Byrd, U.S.N., read by Dr. John H. Finley.

MATTHEW FONTAINE MAURY, naval officer and oceanographer, was born near Fredericksburg, Va., January 14, 1806, and died at Lexington, Va., February 1, 1873. His career included three major voyages, the first on the vessel which took Lafayette back to France, the second around the world aboard the "Vincennes," and the third to the Pacific coast of South America. In 1834 he settled at Fredericksburg with his bride, Ann Hull Herndon. Here he wrote several articles attacking the inefficiency of the Navy, and in the same period produced his authoritative *A New Theoretical and Practical Treatise on Navigation.* A stagecoach accident lamed him permanently, ending his chances of further sea duty. But as superintendent of the new Naval Observatory he revolutionized the recording of oceanographic data. Out of his research on winds and currents came charts of the Atlantic which enabled mariners to lop from 10 to 15 days off the New York–Rio de Janeiro run. Revised charts also reduced the New York–San Francisco sailing time from 180 days to 133 days during the California gold rush. His system was adopted for universal navigation by an international congress at Brussels in 1853. In *The Physical Geography of the Sea* (1855) he established oceanography as a distinct branch of science. He was showered with honors, including a $5,000 purse and silver service from the merchants and underwriters of New York, honorary degrees, and medals from foreign governments. Upon the outbreak of the Civil War he was commissioned a Confederate naval commander. Sent abroad, he was outside the provisions of the amnesty decree at the war's end. He remained outside the country until, four years before his death, he accepted a professorship in meteorology at the Virginia Military Institute at Lexington.

MARIA MITCHELL, astronomer and teacher, was born at Nantucket, Mass., August 1, 1818, and died at Lynn, Mass., June 28, 1889. Her father, an enthusiastic astronomer, taught her to use a telescope. She also assisted him in making mathematical computations by which he rated chronometers for the skippers of whaling vessels. She was, in fact, so precocious in mathematics that she surpassed her school teachers at an early age. With the ending of her formal schooling, she became the town librarian. The Nantucket library had a good collection of scientific works with which she managed to give herself a creditable scientific education in her ample leisure hours. At home during the evenings she continued to watch the heavens, and in October, 1847, she discovered a new comet. Her father sped the news to his scientific friends in Boston, and they passed it along to Europe's learned circles. As a result, Maria received a gold medal from the King of Denmark. Other honors followed: membership in several scientific societies, including the American Academy of Arts and Sciences; a larger telescope, presented by a group of American women; and a position as a computer for the *American Ephemeris and Nautical Almanac*. In 1857 she went abroad for a year to meet and talk with Europe's great men of science. In 1865 Vassar College invited her to become its first professor of astronomy. While she had misgivings about her lack of teaching experience, she accepted. In her lectures and away from them, she was both a guide and an inspiration to her students. In addition, her international reputation helped to win recognition and support for the new girls' college. As a tribute to her teaching ability, educational institutions other than Vassar conferred honorary degrees on her. In 1869 she was elected to the American Philosophical Society.

Every formula which expresses a law of nature is a hymn of praise to God.

Maria Mitchell

[ELECTED IN 1905 BY 48 VOTES]

Bust by Emma F. Brigham; replica unveiled May 20, 1922; gift of William Mitchell Kendall; unveiled by the donor; address by President Henry Noble MacCracken of Vassar College.

The world owes two debts to the science of astronomy: One for its practical uses, and the other for the ideas it has afforded us of the immensity of creation.

Simon Newcomb

[ELECTED IN 1935 BY 78 VOTES]

BUST by Frederick MacMonnies; unveiled May 28, 1936; gift of Dr. Ambrose Swasey, friend of the scientist, who spoke briefly; formal presentation by Dr. Harlow Shapley, Harvard College Observatory; unveiled by Mrs. Emily Newcomb Wilson, daughter of Newcomb, in the absence of his eldest daughter, Dr. Anita Newcomb McGee; address by Dr. William Wallace Campbell, President Emeritus, University of California, and Director Emeritus, Lick Observatory.

SIMON NEWCOMB, astronomer, was born at Wallace, Nova Scotia, March 12, 1835, and died in Washington, D.C., July 11, 1909. He began his distinguished career as a teacher of a country school and there first exhibited his knowledge of higher mathematics. After graduation from the Lawrence Scientific School at Harvard in 1858, he became a computer in the office of the *American Nautical Almanac* at Cambridge, Mass. Later, he became a professor of mathematics in the United States Navy. He was put in charge of a 26-inch equatorial telescope, which was built under his direction. He was director of the *American Nautical Almanac,* professor of mathematics and astronomy at Johns Hopkins, and editor of the *American Journal of Mathematics.* He participated in a number of eclipse expeditions. In 1882 he observed the transit of Venus from an observation point at the Cape of Good Hope. He was retired from the Navy in 1897. As a research associate of the Carnegie Institution of Washington, which financially supported his studies on the motion of the moon, he was able to complete his work and publish his data less than a month before his death. He was president of the American Association for the Advancement of Science in 1877. In 1895 he was elected one of the eight foreign associates of the Paris Academy of Sciences to succeed von Helmholtz; Benjamin Franklin and Louis Agassiz were the only two other Americans so honored. He served two terms as president of the American Mathematical Society. His investigations on the orbits of Uranus, Neptune, and, later, of the inner planets resulted in planetary tables that were adopted almost universally by observatories. Among his books are *The Stars, A Study of the Universe, Side Lights on Astronomy,* and *A Compendium of Spherical Astronomy.*

VI

ENGINEERS, ARCHITECTS

JAMES BUCHANAN EADS, engineer and inventor, was born at Lawrenceburg, Ind., May 23, 1820, and died at Nassau, Bahamas, March 8, 1887. His family settled in St. Louis, Mo. At 13, he left school to help support the family by selling apples on the street and by clerking in a drygoods store. In time he became a purser on a Mississippi river boat and began a career which centered almost entirely on American rivers. After patenting a diving bell, he took a partner and went into the steamboat salvage business. He himself often made dives to the river bottom in the bell. Later he married, sold his interest in the lucrative salvage business, and started a glass manufacturing plant in St. Louis. It failed, leaving him $25,000 in debt. By returning to the salvage and wrecking business he not only paid off his debts but amassed a fortune. He petitioned Congress to authorize the removal of snags and wrecks and to undertake the dredging of the channels of the Mississippi and its tributaries, but to no avail. At the start of the Civil War, Lincoln urgently asked him to help prepare attack and defense plans for the western rivers. Eads built a fleet of seven armor-plated, steam-driven gunboats in an incredibly short time. The first was delivered in 45 days. Six more followed in quick succession. He also converted peacetime vessels, including his own salvage craft, into "tin-clads." The work constituted a vital factor in the military control of the Mississippi. Overwork impaired his health, but he recovered after the war and built the huge steel and masonry bridge across the Mississippi at St. Louis. Later, he persuaded Congress to let him clear a sediment-choked mouth of the Mississippi and to maintain the channel. His expositions on water flow and calculated sediment deposits won him international fame as a hydraulic engineer.

I cannot die; I have not finished my work.

James Buchanan Eads

[ELECTED IN 1920 BY 51 VOTES]

BUST by Charles Grafly; unveiled May 13, 1924; gift of the American Society of Civil Engineers; unveiled by James Eads Switzer, grandson of Captain Eads; address by Dr. George F. Swain, Professor of Civil Engineering at Harvard.

VII

PHYSICIANS, SURGEONS

WILLIAM CRAWFORD GORGAS, physician and sanitary engineer, was born at Toulminville, near Mobile, Ala., October 3, 1854, and died in London, England, July 4, 1920. Unable to attend West Point, he decided to study medicine so that he could join the Army Medical Corps. He received his M.D. degree from Bellevue Hospital Medical College, New York City, in 1879 and was appointed an Army surgeon the next year. Transferred to Fort Brown, Tex., he was summoned to attend the commandant's sister-in-law, Marie Doughty, who had contracted yellow fever. Gorgas himself became a yellow fever victim while looking after Miss Doughty, but both recovered. They were married in 1885. In 1898 he was sent to Havana, Cuba, as chief sanitary officer and subsequently joined Walter Reed and the Yellow Fever Commission. Applying the discoveries of Reed and Carlos J. Finlay, who had traced transmission to the *Aëdes aegypti* mosquito, Gorgas eradicated yellow fever from Havana. When President Theodore Roosevelt appointed his first Panama Canal Commission in 1904, he sent Gorgas to prepare methods of sanitary control. In their abortive attempt to build the canal, the French had lost 22,000 workers from yellow fever and other diseases. Gorgas rid the area of yellow fever, paving the way for completion of the canal. He subsequently made trips to widely separated regions to combat diseases. In 1913 he was called to the Rand Gold Mines in South Africa to wipe out influenza. He also made notable progress in Guayaquil, Ecuador, long plagued by yellow fever. In 1914 he was appointed surgeon general of the Army. He retired from the Army in 1918 and became director of yellow fever research and permanent director of the International Health Board of the Rockefeller Foundation.

If there were no way to control yellow fever and malaria, the hot countries would be left to the inertia of the ages.

William Crawford Gorgas

[ELECTED IN 1950 BY 81 VOTES]

BUST by Bryant Baker; unveiled May 24, 1951; gift of members of the Medical Profession and many other friends of Dr. Gorgas; formal presentation by Dr. Thomas W. Martin, Vice Chairman, Gorgas Hall of Fame Committee and Chairman of the Board, Alabama Power Company; unveiled by Mrs. William D. Wrightson, daughter of Dr. Gorgas; tribute by Dr. Oliver C. Carmichael, Chairman, Gorgas Hall of Fame Committee, and President, The Carnegie Foundation for the Advancement of Teaching. An address was made by Major General Raymond W. Bliss, Surgeon General, Department of the Army. Music for the ceremony by Miss Lucile Cummings and the New York University Chapel Choir.

I leave it to surgeons and physicians to speak the praises of ether in the various operations in which it is now universally used whenever the relief of pain is an object of importance.

William Thomas Green Morton

[ELECTED IN 1920 BY 72 VOTES]

BUST by Helen Farnsworth Mears; replica unveiled May 13, 1924; gift of members of the New York Academy of Medicine; unveiled by Bowditch Morton, grandson of Dr. Morton; address by Dr. William W. Keen, Past-President of the American Surgical Association.

WILLIAM THOMAS GREEN MORTON, dentist and anesthetist, was born in Charlton, Mass., August 9, 1819, and died in New York City, July 15, 1868. He studied dentistry at the College of Dental Surgery in Baltimore and practiced for a time at Farmington, Conn., and in Boston. Dissatisfied with his education, he enrolled at Harvard Medical School in 1844, studying while supporting himself and his new bride, by means of a dental practice. He never received a medical degree. In 1844, at the suggestion of one of his teachers, he used ether in drops as a local anesthetic on a dental patient. On September 30, 1846, when a patient in great pain appeared at his office, Morton administered sulphuric ether by inhalation and painlessly extracted the man's ulcerated tooth. It was the first time ether had been used as a general anesthetic. Later, with Morton supervising the etherization, Dr. John Collins Warren safely and painlessly removed a tumor from the neck of an anesthetized patient at Massachusetts General Hospital in Boston. Other major operations followed, with Morton not only supervising but taking complete responsibility for the success of his anesthetic, which he mysteriously called "letheon" in order to safeguard his secret. He published several papers on techniques and safe dosage. He then sought to patent his discovery as a commercial product, stipulating that "letheon" would be available without cost to certain charitable hospitals. Unsuccessful in obtaining patent rights, he became embittered. When the French Academy of Medicine awarded him, jointly with Prof. Charles T. Jackson, a 5,000-franc prize in recognition of the anesthetic, he rejected it on the ground that the discovery was entirely his. Bills introduced in Congress to vote him $100,000 died in a welter of counterclaims to discovery.

WALTER REED, army surgeon, was born in Gloucester County, Va., September 13, 1851, and died in Washington, D.C., November 22, 1902. Graduated from the University of Virginia Medical School in 1868, he went to the Bellevue Hospital Medical College (later merged with New York University's Medical School) where he received a second M.D. degree a year later. After a brief period in New York he went to Arizona as a U.S. Army surgeon. Here he began his scientific work; but in 1890, realizing that he needed further instruction, he went to Baltimore and studied bacteriology at Johns Hopkins Hospital under the guidance of Dr. William H. Welch. Reed's interest in yellow fever began in 1897, and the following year he was appointed chairman of a committee charged with investigating the causes and means of transmission of typhoid fever, then raging in the army camps. In 1900 there was a serious outbreak of yellow fever among the American troops in Havana, and Reed was placed at the head of a commission of U.S. Army medical officers ordered to investigate the disease. Although the idea of mosquito-borne yellow fever was known as early as 1854, it was Reed who emphasized the importance of experiments with human beings. The work of the commission covered seven months. In 1900, when the commission was established, there were 1,400 cases of yellow fever in Havana; two years later there was not a single case. Reed returned to Washington to resume work at the Army Medical School. Later he became professor of pathology and bacteriology at the Columbia University Medical School. Harvard University conferred on him an honorary A.M. degree, and shortly thereafter the University of Michigan gave him the LL.D. degree. The Army hospital in Washington, D.C., is named for him.

The prayer that has been mine for twenty or more years, that I might be permitted in some way or some time to do something to alleviate human suffering, has been answered.

Walter Reed

[ELECTED IN 1945 BY 49 VOTES]

BUST by Cecil Howard; unveiled May 20, 1948; gift of The American Society of Tropical Medicine and the Officers of the Medical Department, U.S. Army. Contributions were also received from Stephen J. Wigmore, Mrs. Lloyd C. Stickles, and The Foster Hall Collection of the University of Pittsburgh; formal presentation by Dr. Edward I. Salisbury, Medical Director, United Fruit Company; unveiled by Major General Walter L. Reed, U.S.A. [Ret.], son of Walter Reed; a tribute by Major General Raymond W. Bliss, Surgeon General, Department of the Army, was read in his absence by Major General George E. Armstrong, U.S.A. [Ret.], New York University Vice President for Medical Affairs. The principal address was delivered by Dr. Wilbur A. Sawyer, Executive Secretary, Organizing Committee of the Fourth International Congresses on Tropical Medicine and Malaria; music by Miss Gladys Swarthout and the New York University Glee Club.

VIII

INVENTORS

ALEXANDER GRAHAM BELL, inventor of the telephone, was born in Edinburgh, Scotland, March 3, 1847, and died near Baddeck, Nova Scotia, August 2, 1922. His father, Alexander Melville Bell, was the inventor of Visible Speech, a system of symbols depicting the vocal organs in articulating positions. Interested from an early age in the theory of sound, young Bell conceived the idea of the electrical transmission of speech. He made his first experiments with electricity as an instructor at Somersetshire College in Bath, England (1866–67). In 1871 he came to Boston to teach Visible Speech at the Boston School for the Deaf (now the Horace Mann School), and in 1873 was appointed professor of vocal physiology in the School of Oratory at Boston University. Meanwhile, he continued his inventive activities, which benefited from his work with the deaf. Thomas Sanders, the father of one of Bell's deaf pupils, was so impressed by his son's progress that he offered to meet all the expenses of Bell's experimental work on the telephone. With the help of Thomas A. Watson in a shop in Boston, Bell established facts which led to the production of the telephone. On March 10, 1876, he spoke the first words into the completed instrument: "Mr. Watson, come here. I want you!" The first patent was granted to Bell on his 29th birthday, March 3, and was issued to him March 7, 1876 —three days before his complete message was spoken. By October that year he was able to conduct a conversation between Boston and Salem. Litigations followed, but the United States Supreme Court upheld all of Bell's claims to invention. In 1876 Bell married Mabel G. Hubbard, daughter of one of his financial benefactors; he turned his investigative talents to congenital deafness and eugenics. In 1882 Bell became a United States citizen.

All great inventions . . . are the product of many minds. No one man could have made the telephone so practical and so useful.

Alexander Graham Bell

[ELECTED IN 1950 BY 70 VOTES]

BUST by Stanley Martineau; unveiled May 24, 1951; gift of the American Telephone and Telegraph Company; formal presentation by Dr. Oliver E. Buckley, Chairman of the Board, Bell Telephone Laboratories, Inc.; unveiled by Mrs. Gilbert Grosvenor, daughter of Dr. Bell. Address by Dr. Charles F. Kettering, Research Consultant to General Motors and Director of the Corporation.

I trust you for progress. . . . Be as brave as your fathers before you. Have faith! Go forward.

THOMAS ALVA EDISON, inventor of the practical electric light, phonograph, and motion-picture camera, was born in Milan, Ohio, February 11, 1847, and died at Llewellyn Park, West Orange, New Jersey, October 18, 1931. Self-educated, he had read Gibbon's *Decline and Fall of the Roman Empire* and had built a chemical laboratory in his cellar by the time he was 11. In 1862 he saved a station agent's son from death under a train. The grateful father taught Edison telegraphy, an association with electricity that led Edison to experimentation and invention. After five years as a telegrapher in the Midwest, he went to Boston where in 1868 he made his first patented invention, an electrical vote recorder. As a partner in a New York City electrical engineering firm in 1869 Edison invented a stock printer, for which he received $40,000. With the money, his first from an invention, he opened a stock ticker factory in Newark, New Jersey. Later, he built research laboratories, first at Menlo Park, New Jersey, and then at West Orange. He invented the phonograph in 1877 and the motion-picture camera in 1891. On October 21, 1879, he perfected the first feasible incandescent electric lamp. He then developed generating and distribution facilities, paving the way for municipal incandescent lighting and power stations. Edison inaugurated the world's first such system in January, 1882, in London, and America's first later the same year in New York City. After World War I broke out he was appointed president of the Naval Consulting Board, forerunner of the Naval Research Laboratories. Of the 1,097 United States patents issued to Edison during his life, 356 dealt with electric generation, distribution, and lighting.

Thomas Alva Edison

[ELECTED IN 1960 BY 108 VOTES]

BUST by Bryant Baker; unveiled June 4, 1961; gift of Edison Electric Institute on behalf of its members in the investor-owned electric light and power industry throughout the United States; formal presentation by Sherman R. Knapp, President, Edison Electric Institute; unveiled by The Honorable Charles Edison and Mrs. Madeleine Edison Sloane, son and daughter of Thomas Alva Edison; address by General David Sarnoff, Chairman, Radio Corporation of America; tributes and appreciations by Harvey S. Firestone, Jr., Walker L. Cisler, Miss Mary Pickford, Thomas W. Martin, and Dr.-Ing. Giorgio Valerio, of Milan, Italy.

ROBERT FULTON, civil engineer and inventor, was born in Lancaster County, Pa., November 14, 1765, and died in New York City, February 24, 1815. He showed inventive talent at 13 by outfitting a boat with manually operated paddle wheels so that he could fish without poling. Later he turned to painting, first in Philadelphia and then in London. He was painting in Devonshire when his attention was attracted to industrial design by Francis Egerton, Duke of Bridgewater, a canal builder, and Charles, Earl of Stanhope, who later invented the Stanhope printing press. Under their influence, Fulton patented a device to raise or lower a boat from one canal system to another. Impressed with the possibilities of canal development, he wrote a treatise on its advantages and sent copies to George Washington, then President. He took out patents for several other industrial inventions, among them a canal dredging machine, a flax-spinning machine, and a device for sawing marble. In France, in 1797, he succeeded in interesting Napoleon in the military possibilities of a submarine and a torpedo. The submarine, the "Nautilus," made a good impression in trials at Le Havre. Napoleon authorized Fulton to hunt down British warships; the reward was to be proportional to the size of the ship, up to 400,000 francs for a 30-cannon frigate. But as time passed and the "Nautilus" failed to sink any English ships, Napoleon lost interest. Under the auspices of the American minister to France, Fulton also built a steamboat. Launched on the Seine in 1803, it promptly broke in two and sank. Outfitted with a new hull, it stayed afloat but scarcely moved. Still, Fulton was so encouraged that he ordered a steam engine built for yet another try. On August 17, 1807, the "Clermont" made its historic New York-Albany round trip on the Hudson in 62 hours.

To direct the genius and resources of our country to useful improvements, to the sciences, the arts, education, the amendment of the public mind and morals, in such pursuits lie real honor and the nation's glory.

Robert Fulton

[ELECTED IN 1900 BY 86 VOTES]

BUST by Jean-Antoine Houdon; replica unveiled September 29, 1909; donor unknown.

Be it known that I have invented a new and useful machine for sewing seams in cloth and other articles requiring to be sewed, and I do hereby declare a full and exact description thereof.

Elias Howe

[ELECTED IN 1915 BY 61 VOTES]

BUST by Charles Keck; unveiled May 8, 1930; gift of admirers of the inventor's services to women; unveiled by Elias Howe's granddaughter, Mrs. Eustis L. Hopkins; address by Miss Frances Perkins, Industrial Commissioner of the State of New York.

ELIAS HOWE, inventor of the practical sewing machine, was born at Spencer, Mass., July 9, 1819, and died in Brooklyn, N.Y., October 3, 1867. When he was 12 his impoverished parents hired him out to a farmer in exchange for his board and clothing. In 1835 he went to Lowell, Mass., as an apprentice in a shop which manufactured looms. It was here that he first observed the principle of the shuttle which he was to use later in the sewing machine. He next worked in a Cambridge machine shop, operating a hemp-carding machine. Moving to Boston, he became an assistant to Ari Davis, a maker of watches and scientific instruments for the Harvard faculty. The experience developed his natural skill with machinery. Shortly after he married Elizabeth J. Ames in 1841, he began his first attempts to make a sewing machine. His first—a failure—was based in principle on the motions of hand sewing. But his second, embodying the shuttle principle, looked so promising that he gave up his job to work on it full-time. His partner, George Fisher, advanced $500 toward tools, and his father provided the Howe family with a place to live. In 1845 Howe produced a model which sewed 250 stitches a minute and, with its eye-pointed needle and lock-stitch construction, it was the ancestor of today's sewing machines. This model exceeded the speed of five hand sewers. In 1846 he constructed a second machine and was granted a patent. His third machine was sold for £250 in England to a manufacturer who also received the entire rights for Great Britain. During the next few years Howe scarcely made enough to keep alive, but after a legal clarification of his patent rights his royalties rose to as much as $4,000 weekly. During the Civil War he used the royalties to support a Union regiment in which he served as a private.

SAMUEL FINLEY BREESE MORSE, inventor and artist, was born at Charlestown, Mass., April 27, 1791, and died in New York City, April 2, 1872. While at Yale, he showed talent as a painter. Encouraged toward an art career by Gilbert Stuart and others, he forgot his college interest in electricity and sailed for England to study painting. As his talent matured, he won prizes and exhibited paintings in the Royal Academy. He returned to Boston and opened a studio, where he was a successful portraitist. Among his best portraits are two of Lafayette, painted in 1825; today the New York Public Library owns one and the City of New York owns the other. He was a founder and first president of the National Academy of Design. The death of his wife, his father, and his mother in less than four years greatly changed his life. He returned to Europe for three years. On his voyage home, a chance conversation with another passenger, Charles Thomas Jackson, drew from Morse the observation that it probably would be possible to transmit intelligence by electricity. Stimulated by his own suggestion, he sketched the first model of a telegraph. He became a professor of Fine Arts at New York University (1832), and invented the recording telegraph in one of the buildings of the University on Washington Square. The instrument went through several modifications before Morse filed for a patent in 1837. "Morse code" also was modified before it reached its present form. Morse originally had intended his invention for secret communications and had drawn up a code so elaborate that it required a huge dictionary. The first telegraph line was built between Washington and Baltimore. On May 24, 1844, Morse sent from the Supreme Court room in the Capitol to Alfred Vail, his partner, in Baltimore, the message: "What hath God wrought!"

I am persuaded that whatever facilitates intercourse between the different portions of the human family will have the effect under the guidance of sound moral principles to promote the best interests of man.

Samuel Finley Breese Morse

[ELECTED IN 1900 BY 82 VOTES]

BUST by Chester Beach; unveiled May 10, 1928; gift of The Morse Hall of Fame Memorial Committee; presented by Richard E. Enright, former Commissioner of Police, New York City, and Chairman of the Committee; unveiled by Miss Leila Livingston Morse, granddaughter of the inventor; addresses by Dr. John H. Finley, President of the American Geographical Society; Professor Frank Jewett Mather, Jr., of the department of Art and Archaeology, Princeton University, and Cass Gilbert, President of the National Academy of Design. A letter concerning Morse from Nikola Tesla was read. A hymn, "What Hath God Wrought," written by Dr. Robert Underwood Johnson, was also read, and music written for it by Dr. Henry Hadley was played by the Gloria Trumpeters.

If someday they say of me that in my work I have contributed something to the welfare and happiness of my fellow men, I shall be satisfied.

George Westinghouse

[ELECTED IN 1955 BY 62 VOTES]

BUST by Edmondo Quattrocchi; unveiled December 1, 1957; gift of the American Society of Mechanical Engineers through a legacy from Herman Westinghouse, a brother, and contributions from the American Institute of Electrical Engineers, American Society for Engineering Education, Engineers Joint Council, Westinghouse Electric Corporation, and Westinghouse Air Brake Company; formal presentation by William F. Ryan, President, The American Society of Mechanical Engineers; unveiled by Walter J. Barrett, President, American Institute of Electrical Engineers; address by the Hon. Herbert Hoover, former President of the United States.

GEORGE WESTINGHOUSE, inventor, engineer, and manufacturer, was born at Central Bridge, N.Y., October 6, 1846, and died in New York City, March 12, 1914. The son of an inventor and farm machinery manufacturer, he acquired an early taste for mechanics. At 15 he tried unsuccessfully to enlist for the Civil War, but later he served as a cavalry scout and a naval engineer. When he was 19 he obtained his first patent for a small rotary engine and three years later invented the air brake, a boon to railroads. The same year the Westinghouse Air Brake Company was organized. He turned next to organizing a company which developed a complete railroad switch and signal system. In 1885 he began work on alternating electrical current, an area which was unexplored at the time. In this period the Westinghouse Electric Corporation was established and, in 1886, Great Barrington, Mass., glowed with light from the first alternating current transformer system in the United States. By 1895, the first generators were operating at Niagara and the following year Buffalo was receiving power from them. In succeeding years Westinghouse organized numerous companies for the development of his inventions, some of which were a motor for trolley cars, an electrically operated brake for subway trains, shock absorbers for automobiles, and apparatus for improvement of locomotive electrification. As a youth, Westinghouse had said: "If I ever become an employer, I'll give everyone Saturday afternoon for a holiday." In 1871 he made good this promise in all his shops. He also gave his employees vacations with pay —an unheard of benefit at that time. In 1890, when the Westinghouse Air Brake Company moved from Allegheny to Wilmerding, Pa., he established for his employees model shops and hundreds of model houses at low prices.

ELI WHITNEY, inventor, was born at Westboro, Mass., December 8, 1765, and died in New Haven, Conn., January 8, 1825. He put himself through Yale by teaching school and by repairing equipment around the college. He used tools so skillfully that it was remarked that a good mechanic had been lost to the trade when Whitney went to college. After graduation, Whitney accepted a position as a tutor in Georgia. Aboard ship he met Mrs. Nathanael Greene, the Revolutionary War general's widow, who—when Whitney arrived in Savannah to learn that the tutorial post had been filled—offered him living quarters on her plantation. To repay her hospitality, he repaired and maintained plantation equipment. One evening he heard a group of planters deploring the fact that, while much land was suitable only for short- and medium-staple cotton, it was economically hazardous to grow the crop because of the labor required to separate seed from lint. Whitney built a machine which would turn out 50 pounds of cleaned cotton a day, and shortly thereafter went into partnership with Mrs. Greene's estate manager, Phineas Miller, to build cotton gins. However, before they had established clear patent rights, imitators had put other models on the market. It was 1807 before a United States court decision ruled in favor of the Whitney gin. Then, when he applied five years later for a patent renewal, his application was refused. Thus it was not the cotton gin but a small-arms factory he set up later that gave him a measure of financial success. Nevertheless, the cotton gin's impact on the economy of the South was tremendous. In 1792, just before Whitney invented the first crude gin, the United States exported 138,328 pounds of cotton; at the turn of the century, the figure had reached 17,-790,000 pounds.

The machine, it is true, operates in the first instance, on mere physical elements, to produce an accumulation and distribution of property. But do not all the arts of civilization follow in its train?

Eli Whitney

[ELECTED IN 1900 BY 69 VOTES]

BUST by Chester Beach; unveiled May 12, 1926; gift of the New York Cotton Exchange; unveiled by Miss Frances Edwards Chaplain, granddaughter of Whitney; address by Professor Henry W. Farnham of Yale University.

Wilbur Wright

[ELECTED IN 1955 BY 86 VOTES]

[BUST has not yet been unveiled.]

WILBUR WRIGHT, airplane inventor, was born at Millville, near New Castle, Ind., April 16, 1867, and died in Dayton, Ohio, May 30, 1912. Early in life he and his brother, Orville, published a weekly newspaper on a printing press Orville had built. Later, the brothers organized the Wright Cycle Company and manufactured a bicycle with some success. They became interested in aeronautics in 1896 and read everything they could find on the subject. Three years later Wilbur built his first model biplane, which he flew as a kite. With the help of the Weather Bureau, the brothers selected Kitty Hawk, N.C., for glider experiments. After several experimental flights, they built a wind tunnel in Dayton for more accurate testing. By December, 1903, they had completed a machine with a four-cylinder motor. Returning to Kill Devil Hill at Kitty Hawk, they took the plane aloft on December 17. Orville made the first successful powered flight—a 12-second hop that ended 120 feet from the starting point. The same day Wilbur, on the fourth flight, traveled some 852 feet and remained in the air nearly a minute. During the next three years the brothers made 160 flights, one covering 24 miles in 38 minutes. In May, 1906, they received a patent for the airplane. The War Department showed no interest in the machine until after Wilbur had gained European admiration with a demonstration flight near Le Mans and had arranged for a French syndicate to build the machine in France. During the Hudson-Fulton celebration in 1909, he returned to New York City and flew from Governors Island to the Statue of Liberty and to Grant's Tomb and back. Soon afterward the American Wright Company was organized, with Wilbur as its head. He died of typhoid fever just as he was beginning to win recognition for his part in airplane development.

IX

MISSIONARIES, EXPLORERS

DANIEL BOONE, frontiersman and explorer, was born in Berks County, Pa., November 2, 1734, and died in what is now St. Charles County, Mo., September 26, 1820. He achieved fame as a hunter while still in his teens. He explored parts of the Blue Ridge Mountains in 1750 and during the next few years continued his explorations in what we now know as North Carolina, South Carolina, Tennessee, and Kentucky. His work among the Indians opened much of the region to pioneer settlement. During the French and Indian Wars he participated in the battle of July 9, 1755, against the Indians at Fort Duquesne. Here Braddock was mortally wounded and more than 700 officers and men were killed. Boone narrowly escaped on a horse. The next year he married Rebeccah Bryan of North Carolina. His next fighting was against the Cherokees. When peace had been restored he set out with his brother to explore the territory through Georgia to Pensacola, Fla. He also made several other expeditions, and on several occasions his party was attacked by Indians. In 1774 he and a companion covered 800 miles of wilderness in 62 days to rescue a band of men from an impending Indian attack. During the Revolutionary War the Indians carried off his daughter and two other girls. After two days of tracking, Boone and six other men overtook the raiding party and rescued the prisoners. Shortly afterward, he himself was taken prisoner by Indians; after four months of captivity he managed to escape. Defective titles cost him much of the land that he had explored and claimed. However, Congressional action saved his last home, a log cabin, in what is now Missouri. So far as is known, the only contemporary portrait of Boone was done by Chester Harding in the frontiersman's old age. It hangs in the Kentucky statehouse at Frankfort.

May the same Almighty Goodness which has turned a cruel war into peace banish the accursed monster War from all lands.

Daniel Boone

[ELECTED IN 1915 BY 52 VOTES]

BUST by Albin Polasek; unveiled May 12, 1926; gift of the Boone Family Association; unveiled by Jesse P. Crump, descendant of Boone; address written by the Vice-President of the United States, Hon. Charles G. Dawes, and read by the Director of the Hall of Fame.

X

THE MILITARY

DAVID GLASGOW FARRAGUT, naval officer, was born near Knoxville, Tenn., July 5, 1801, and died at Portsmouth, N.H., August 14, 1870. The son of a naval officer, he was adopted after his mother's death by a family friend, David Porter, then commanding the New Orleans naval station. Appointed a midshipman at nine, young Farragut sailed under Porter aboard the "Essex" the following year. In the War of 1812 Farragut sailed the Pacific aboard the "Essex" as captain's aide, quarter gunner, and powder boy. In one naval engagement, he was put in command of a captured vessel and sailed it into a Chilean port. Later, he was taken prisoner but was exchanged. During his sea duty he was tutored by Charles Folsom, later American consul to Tunis. Farragut also attended lectures at Yale while stationed there in 1826. He served in the Mexican War and in 1854 established the navy yard at Mare Island, California; he commanded it for four years. During the Civil War he was given command of a squadron with orders to neutralize the two forts guarding the Confederate harbor of New Orleans. His 17 ships and mortar flotilla vainly bombarded Forts Jackson and St. Philip. At last, he gave orders to run by them; the maneuver was successful. He then defeated a Confederate flotilla above the forts and, on April 25, 1862, reached New Orleans, which surrendered without bloodshed. He employed the "run-by" tactic again in support of General Grant's Vicksburg campaign. On August 5, 1864, he put a stop to blockade running at Mobile Bay, a chief source of Confederate supplies, by sailing past an enemy flotilla and a double row of mines, then called "torpedoes." It was on this occasion that he shouted his inspirational cry: "Damn the torpedoes! Go ahead!" Two years later, the rank of admiral was created especially for him.

As to being prepared for defeat, I certainly am not. Any man who is prepared for defeat would be half defeated before he commenced. I hope for success, shall do all in my power to secure it, and trust to God for the rest.

David Glasgow Farragut

[ELECTED IN 1900 BY 79 VOTES]

BUST by Charles Grafly; unveiled May 5, 1927; gift of members of the Naval Order of the United States and other citizens; presented by Colonel Robert M. Thompson, Honorary President of the Navy League; unveiled by Captain Farragut F. Hall, great-nephew of the Admiral; address by Rear-Admiral Bradley A. Fiske, U.S.N. [Ret.]

I determined, first, to use the greatest number of troops practicable; second, to hammer continuously against the enemy until by mere attrition, if in no other way, there should be nothing left to him but submission.

Ulysses Simpson Grant

[ELECTED IN 1900 BY 93 VOTES]

BUST by James Earle Fraser with Thomas Hudson Jones; unveiled May 22, 1923; gift of citizens; unveiled, with address, by Major-General J. G. Hubbard, U.S.A. [Ret.] D.S.M. This bust replaced a former one, by Henry M. Shrady; unveiled April 27, 1922, by Marshal Joseph-Jacques-Césaire Joffre, and Major U. S. Grant 3d, U.S.A.

ULYSSES SIMPSON GRANT, commander in chief of the Union Army and eighteenth President of the United States, was born at Point Pleasant, Ohio, April 27, 1822, and died at Mount McGregor, N.Y., July 23, 1885. He was graduated from West Point in 1843 and served with distinction during the Mexican War. He resigned his commission in 1854 and tried unsuccessfully to adjust to civilian life. He was a clerk in a leather store run by his brothers at Galena, Ill., when the Civil War broke out. He applied for a commission and was made colonel of the 21st Illinois Volunteers in June, 1861. His rise was rapid; within three months he became a brigadier general. His first victories, the capture of Fort Henry on the Tennessee River and Fort Donelson on the Cumberland, won him the rank of major general of volunteers. He successfully prosecuted the Civil War to its end, first as supreme commander in the West after October, 1863, and finally as commander in chief of the Union Army after March, 1864. His surrender terms to General Robert E. Lee at Appomattox Court House were generous. Grant forestalled a movement for Lee's arrest by declaring that such an action would violate the surrender terms. Grant, the Republican candidate, won the Presidency over the Democrats' Horatio Seymour in 1868. Grant was backed by those who sought a punitive reconstruction policy in the South and those who sought personal gains through his influence. His two terms were blemished by scandals involving persons whom he trusted. Bankrupt and ill of throat cancer, he struggled in retirement to finish his *Personal Memoirs* to provide an income for his family. He succeeded in completing these two volumes of military history only four days before he died. He and his wife, Julia, lie in an imposing tomb in New York City.

THOMAS JONATHAN "STONEWALL" JACKSON, military officer, was born in Clarksburg, Va. (now West Virginia), January 21, 1824, and died at Chancellorsville, near Fredericksburg, Va., May 10, 1863. Educated in a small country school and reared by a devoted uncle, he was graduated from West Point in 1846. He served with distinction in the Mexican War, and afterward taught artillery tactics for ten years at the Virginia Military Institute in Lexington. He returned from a European trip in 1856 to find that war, which he called the "sum of all evils," was impending. When Virginia seceded in April, 1861, the Lexington cadets were ordered to Richmond with Jackson in command of the corps. Later he was sent to Harper's Ferry as a colonel of infantry and achieved such notable success that he was promoted to the rank of brigadier general. At the first Battle of Bull Run, Jackson earned his nickname when Brigadier General Barnard E. Bee exclaimed: "There is Jackson standing like a stone wall!" Promoted to major general, Jackson next distinguished himself as a strategist in the Shenandoah Valley campaign. He served with Lee in the spring of 1862 and was so successful in subsequent campaigns that Lee was able to advance into Union territory and defeat General McClellan's advance on Richmond. In April, 1863, Jackson—now a lieutenant general—rejoined Lee to ward off Union troops advancing on Fredericksburg. For many months his corps bore the brunt of battle; but his engagement at Chancellorsville, one of the most stubborn of the war, was his greatest triumph. He had just forced the Union Army into retreat, when, while inspecting his positions, he was mortally wounded by accidental gunfire from his own troops. He died a few days later and, in accordance with his wishes, was buried at Lexington.

You may be whatever you resolve to be. . . .
Never take counsel of your fears.

Thomas Jonathan "Stonewall" Jackson

[ELECTED IN 1955 BY 72 VOTES]

BUST by Bryant Baker; unveiled May 19, 1957; gift of the United Daughters of the Confederacy; unveiled by Mrs. E. Randolph Preston and Mrs. J. B. McAfee, granddaughter and great-granddaughter of General Jackson, with the great-great-granddaughters, Julia McAfee, Trudy Shaffner, and Juliana Christian Creech; formal presentation by Miss Edna Howard Fowler, President-General, United Daughters of the Confederacy; an expression of appreciation by Mrs. L. M. Bashinsky, Chairman, U.D.C.-General Jackson Hall of Fame Committee; principal address by the Hon. Wilber M. Brucker, Secretary of the Army, U.S.A.

He hath made the flag of America respected among the flags of other nations.

John Paul Jones

[ELECTED IN 1925 BY 68 VOTES]

BUST by Charles Grafly; unveiled May 10, 1928; gift of the Grand Lodge F. & A. M., New York; presented by the Most Worshipful John A. Dutton, Grand Master of Masons in the State of New York; unveiled by Rear-Admiral Richmond Pearson Hobson, U.S.N. [Ret.]; address by Rear-Admiral Willard H. Brownson, U.S.N. [Ret.]

JOHN PAUL JONES, naval officer, was born in Kirkcudbrightshire, Scotland, July 6, 1747, and died in Paris, July 18, 1792. Born John Paul, he went to sea at the age of 12. Several years later, commanding a ship off Tobago in the West Indies, he was forced to kill a crew member during a mutiny. On the advice of friends, he disappeared to avoid standing trial before hostile witnesses. He added "Jones" to his name and settled in Philadelphia. At the beginning of the Revolution he was commissioned a lieutenant in the Continental Navy. After many delays, he was given command of the "Ranger" and began raiding the British coast. In 1778 he captured the "Drake," the first British warship to surrender to an American vessel. He made his headquarters in Paris; and while his exploits were scarcely known in the United States, Jones was a hero in the scientific, political, and diplomatic circles which centered on Benjamin Franklin, the American ambassador. Jones renamed his next ship, a rebuilt French merchantman, the "Bonhomme Richard" in honor of Franklin's *Poor Richard.* On September 23, 1779, the "Richard" sighted the British man-of-war "Serapis" with a convoy of merchantmen. Jones sailed the "Richard" alongside the "Serapis," lashed the ships together, and ordered his crew into hand-to-hand combat. The battle continued into the night, illuminated by fires that raged throughout the "Bonhomme Richard." Seeing that the American vessel was doomed, the British commander asked Jones if he was ready to surrender. "I've just begun to fight!" Jones shouted back. Not long afterward, the Americans swarmed aboard the "Serapis." The British surrendered. On his return to the United States in 1781, Jones was hailed as a hero and formally thanked by Congress.

ROBERT EDWARD LEE, commander in chief of the Confederate Army, was born at Stratford, Westmoreland County, Va., January 19, 1807, and died in Lexington, Va., October 12, 1870. He was graduated from West Point second in his class in 1829. Two years later he married Mary Ann Randolph Custis, a great-granddaughter of Martha Washington. He served with distinction in the Mexican War and was superintendent at West Point from 1852 to 1855. At the outbreak of the Civil War, he was offered the field command of the United States Army. Devoted to the Union and not then a secessionist, he faced a great personal conflict. When the Virginia convention voted secession he turned down the proffered command and resigned from the army, feeling that he could not bear arms against his home state. He was made a Confederate general and designated military adviser to President Jefferson Davis. When Joseph E. Johnston was wounded at Fair Oaks, Lee assumed command of the Army of Northern Virginia. In the months that followed he became a rallying point for the morale of the Confederacy and, through his genius for strategy, won many battles in which he was far outnumbered in men, artillery, and equipment. His sound logistics, keen analysis of military intelligence, and willingness to fight against odds made him one of the best commanders of all time. The war already had been lost to the South when Lee was designated general in chief on February 6, 1865. Finally overwhelmed, he surrendered the remnants of his armies to General Grant at Appomattox Court House in April, 1865. After the war he became president of Washington College, now Washington and Lee University. Under his guidance it became one of the South's outstanding schools. He died admired by both North and South.

There is a true glory and a true honor: the glory of duty done—the honor of the integrity of principle.

Robert Edward Lee

[ELECTED IN 1900 BY 68 VOTES]

BUST by George T. Brewster; unveiled May 22, 1923; gift of the N. Y. Division of the United Daughters of the Confederacy; unveiled by Dr. George Bolling Lee, grandson of the General; address by Hon. Martin W. Littleton, President of the Southern Society of New York.

War is cruelty and you cannot refine it. I want peace and believe it can only be reached through union and war, and I will ever conduct war with a view to perfect and early success.

William Tecumseh Sherman

[ELECTED IN 1905 BY 58 VOTES]

BUST by Augustus Saint-Gaudens; replica unveiled May 21, 1925; gift of the Union Society of the Civil War and of the Army and Navy Club of America; unveiled by P. Tecumseh Sherman, son of the General; address by General John J. Pershing, General of the Armies of the United States [Ret.].

WILLIAM TECUMSEH SHERMAN, Union Army officer, was born at Lancaster, Ohio, February 8, 1820, and died in New York City, February 14, 1891. He was graduated from West Point in 1840 and spent several years in Southern garrisons. During the Mexican War he served in California. He resigned from the army to seek a career, first as a banker and then as a lawyer. Rebuffed in attempts to rejoin the army, he accepted the superintendency of a new military academy near Alexandria, La. (now Louisiana State University). He resigned when Louisiana seceded, and in May, 1861, he rejoined the expanding United States Army as a colonel. Promotions came rapidly. He commanded a brigade at Bull Run, a division at Shiloh, and the 15th Corps at Vicksburg. After Vicksburg surrendered, he was made a brigadier general of regulars. When General Grant became supreme commander in the spring of 1864, Sherman replaced him as commander of the western armies. The most widely known episode of his career occurred late in 1864 when he attacked, occupied, and burned much of Atlanta. Then, with some 60,000 men, he marched through the virtually undefended countryside to Savannah, destroying supplies, crops, and any civilian property which might help the Confederate cause. Savannah fell on December 21. Sherman was challenged in North Carolina by Joseph E. Johnston, Confederate commander in the Carolinas. Suddenly, Johnston heard of Lee's surrender at Appomattox and asked Sherman for terms. Sherman offered him such generous ones that they might be interpreted as a plan for rebuilding the devastated area. This gesture, however, was blocked by Secretary of War Stanton. When Grant became President in 1869, Sherman succeeded him as commander in chief of the Army.

XI

LAWYERS, JUDGES

RUFUS CHOATE, lawyer, was born at Hog Island, Essex County, Mass., October 1, 1799, and died in Halifax, Nova Scotia, July 13, 1859. A precocious child, he read *The Pilgrim's Progress* at six, and before he was ten he had exhausted the reading material in the village library. Determined to have a college education, he borrowed money to put himself through Dartmouth. He was valedictorian in the graduating class of 1819. Daniel Webster's brilliant handling of the famous Dartmouth case evoked Choate's highest admiration, and he decided to make law his career. He was admitted to the bar in 1822 and opened an office at Danvers, Mass. Throughout his life he was called into public service from time to time, but he was a reluctant servant. He had little lasting influence as a statesman—a role to which he was indifferent. His chief interest was law. He was primarily a courtroom lawyer whose cases were, for the most part, tried before juries. His fame rests on his dramatic performances in pleading his cases. One of the great orators of American legal history, he had a sweeping command of language, a penetrating logical faculty, and a pragmatic, persuasive manner in courtroom presentation. He was a profound scholar who searched assiduously for precedents and neglected no detail in preparing for a courtroom appearance. When his idol, Webster, died in 1852, Choate worked long and earnestly preparing a eulogy which he delivered in August, 1853, at Dartmouth, the alma mater of both men. Choate served in the United States House of Representatives and later succeeded Daniel Webster in the United States Senate. Among his principal Congressional speeches were those dealing with the Oregon boundary, the tariff, the fiscal bank bill, the Smithsonian Institution, and the annexation of Texas.

The profession of the Bar has seemed to possess a two-fold nature. It has resisted despotism and yet taught obedience. It has recognized the rights of man, and yet has reckoned it always the most sacred of those rights to be shielded and led by the divine nature and immortal reason of law.

Rufus Choate

[ELECTED IN 1915 BY 52 VOTES]

BUST by Hermon A. MacNeil; unveiled May 10, 1928; gift of members of the Association of the Bar of the City of New York and of Richard T. Crane; presented by Henry D. Williams, representing the Association; unveiled by the Misses Helen and Priscilla Choate, relatives of Rufus Choate; address by Hon. Joseph M. Proskauer, Associate Justice of the Appellate Division of the Supreme Court, First Department, New York.

We ought not to separate the science of public law from that of ethics. States or bodies politic are to be considered as moral persons having a public will capable and free to do right and wrong.

James Kent

[ELECTED IN 1900 BY 65 VOTES]

BUST by Edmond T. Quinn; unveiled May 12, 1926; gift of the New York State Bar Association; unveiled by Mrs. Knowlton, granddaughter of Kent; address by the late Alton B. Parker, read by Hon. Samuel H. Ordway, formerly Justice of the Supreme Court of New York.

JAMES KENT, jurist and legal commentator, was born in Putnam County, N.Y., July 31, 1763, and died in New York City, December 12, 1847. He received his B.A. from Yale in 1781. At college he read *Blackstone's Commentaries* and, though only 15, was so impressed that he decided to become a lawyer. After his apprenticeship in the law office of Attorney-General Egbert Benson in Poughkeepsie, N.Y., Kent was admitted to the New York Supreme Court bar at 21, married Elizabeth Bailey, and entered into a law partnership. His political course was set during this period by his admiration for Alexander Hamilton and by his association with Federalist leaders who came to Poughkeepsie in 1788 for the constitutional convention. He ran for Congress in 1793 but was defeated. The same year, he moved to New York City, where he became Columbia College's first professor of law. His activities in state politics led to an appointment to the New York Supreme Court bench in 1798. He moved to Albany and in 1804 became the court's chief judge. He helped to institute the practice of handing down written opinions in the New York Supreme Court. In 1814 he became chancellor of the New York Court of Chancery and helped to strengthen that formerly uninfluential body. Retired at the age of 60, he returned briefly to the law professorship at Columbia. At 63, he began to rewrite and expand his lectures into what ultimately became his *Commentaries on American Law,* a monumental work that included treatises on international, commercial, maritime, and American constitutional law. The section on international law is the first general American work on that subject. A stout conservative, he once was characterized as a man who firmly believed in "the rights of the individual as distinguished from those of the people."

JOHN MARSHALL, fourth chief justice of the United States, was born in what is now Fauquier County, Va., September 24, 1755, and died in Philadelphia, July 6, 1835. As a young man he left the wilderness of Virginia to become an officer in the Revolution and to attend lectures by George Wythe at William and Mary College. He was admitted to the bar in 1780 and practiced law in his home county until he was elected a delegate to the Virginia Assembly. At the Virginia ratifying convention he defended the new United States Constitution, the document which was to become the focal point of his life. He was made chief justice of the United States Supreme Court in 1801 while serving as Secretary of State under John Adams. During his long tenure on the bench he made several important strides toward establishing the Constitution's power over state and federal laws. He regarded the Constitution as an instrument of national unity —clear and precise, yet subject to broadening interpretations. A keen Federalist, he often quarreled with Jefferson. Their conflict reached its height when Marshall, as presiding circuit judge in the Aaron Burr case, interpreted treason to mean an overt act rather than a conspiracy. Owing to this interpretation, Burr escaped conviction as a traitor. Many of the most brilliant lawyers of the day testified in Marshall's courtroom, among them Daniel Webster. Marshall's keen wit and great charm made even his enemies admire him. During his 34 years as chief justice he rarely relied on judicial precedent; his opinions, written in clear and precise style, were a series of deductions from a self-evident premise. Early in his career he went to Paris as an envoy to help settle difficulties with the French during the threat of war that stemmed from the XYZ Affair. He was a loyal supporter of John Adams.

The Constitution and the laws made in pursuance thereof are supreme; they control the constitutions and laws of the respective States and cannot be controlled by them.

John Marshall

[ELECTED IN 1900 BY 91 VOTES]

BUST by Herbert Adams; unveiled May 21, 1925; gift of the Members of the Association of the Bar of the City of New York; unveiled by W. W. Braxton, great-grandson of the Chief Justice; tribute by radio, by Hon. William Howard Taft, Chief Justice of the United States and former President of the United States; address by Hon. John W. Davis, former Ambassador to Great Britain and former President of the American Bar Association.

The founders of the Constitution, with profound wisdom, laid the corner-stone of our national republic in the permanent independence of the judicial establishment.

Joseph Story

[ELECTED IN 1900 BY 64 VOTES]

BUST by Herbert Adams; unveiled May 8, 1930; gift of American jurists and lawyers; unveiled by Hon. Martin T. Manton, senior Circuit Judge, U.S. Circuit Court of Appeals; address by Hon. John Bassett Moore, member of the Permanent Court of Arbitration at The Hague and formerly judge of the Permanent Court of International Justice.

JOSEPH STORY, jurist, was born in Marblehead, Mass., September 8, 1779, and died in Cambridge, Mass., September 10, 1845. At 15 he began to study in preparation for college, and in 1795 he entered Harvard. After a grinding study routine that undermined his health, he was graduated second in the 1798 class. He continued his law studies at Marblehead and Salem, where he was admitted to the bar in 1801 and opened a law office. A staunch Republican, he began taking an active role in public affairs. Because he was highly regarded as an orator, he was chosen by Marblehead to deliver the eulogy on the death of Washington. Salem sent him to the Massachusetts legislature as its representative from 1805 to 1807. In 1808 he was elected to Congress for a year to fill an unexpired term, but he declined re-election. He was bitterly against slavery and frequently condemned it from the bench. On November 18, 1811, at the age of 32, he was appointed an associate justice of the United States Supreme Court, the youngest jurist ever to hold the office, which at that time included circuit court duties. The War of 1812 flooded his circuit court with cases stemming from privateering. His decisions in these cases put the admiralty jurisdiction of the federal courts on a sound basis. He moved to Cambridge in 1829 to accept the newly created law professorship at Harvard. Outstanding not only as a teacher but as an organizer, he might almost be considered the founder of the Harvard Law School. His *Commentaries* began appearing in 1832 and thereafter came out volume after volume in rapid succession. These works, together with his other legal writings, are said to have brought him the handsome sum of $10,000 yearly. Even before the appearance of his *Commentaries,* he was known and respected in British legal circles for his decisions.

XII

STATESMEN

JOHN ADAMS, second President of the United States, was born at Braintree (now Quincy), Mass., October 30, 1735, and died there July 4, 1826. He was graduated from Harvard in 1755. In pre-Revolutionary days he went to Boston where he was active in patriotic circles and became a leader in opposing the Stamp Act. He was a delegate to the first and second Continental Congresses. As a member of the Declaration of Independence drafting committee, he raised an eloquent voice in favor of that document. To bind Virginia to the Revolutionary movement, he seconded the nomination of George Washington, a Virginian, as commander in chief of the Army. Beginning in 1779 Adams visited Europe on various diplomatic missions. During these years he succeeded in getting a much-needed loan from the Netherlands for the United States. He helped draw up the Treaty of Paris which ended the American Revolution. He then became the first United States minister to Great Britain, but negotiations with the former enemy became so difficult that after three years he asked to be recalled. Throughout Washington's administration he served as Vice-President, acting as a moderator between the clashing policies and personalities of Hamilton and Jefferson. After his election to the presidency in 1796, Adams followed some of the policies of Hamilton, a pro-British Federalist. However, Adams safely steered American policy away from war with France when American Federalists were outraged over the incident known as the XYZ Affair. Through diplomacy, Adams settled the matter without war. Defeated by Jefferson in the 1800 presidential election, Adams retired to Quincy, where, as a highly respected elder statesman and leader of the loyal opposition to President Jefferson, he continued to issue statements on American policy.

As a government so popular can be supported only by universal knowledge and virtue, it is the duty of all ranks to promote the means of education as well as true religion, purity of manners, and integrity of life.

John Adams

[ELECTED IN 1900 BY 62 VOTES]

BUST by John Francis Paramino; unveiled May 13, 1924; gift of the Massachusetts Society of the Sons of the Revolution; unveiled by John Adams, great-great-grandson of President Adams; address by Professor William M. Sloane, President of the American Academy of Arts and Letters.

I live in the faith and hope of the progressive advancement of Christian liberty and expect to abide by the same in death.

John Quincy Adams

[ELECTED IN 1905 BY 60 VOTES]

BUST by Edmond T. Quinn; unveiled May 8, 1930; gift of a gentleman of New York, for the American Historical Association; unveiled by Henry L. Abbott, great-great-grandson of the President; address by Hon. Frederick H. Gillett, U.S. Senator from Massachusetts, formerly Speaker of the House of Representatives.

JOHN QUINCY ADAMS, sixth President of the United States, was born at Braintree (now Quincy), Mass., July 11, 1767, and died in Washington, D.C., February 23, 1848. As a youth he accompanied his father, John Adams, on diplomatic missions to Europe. He also visited Russia with Francis Dana, sent as America's envoy but rejected by the imperial court. Adams entered Harvard and was graduated in 1787. Under President Washington he was minister to the Netherlands. During the following administration, his father's, he spent four years as minister to Berlin. He was elected a Federalist senator on his return to the United States. But his support of the Embargo Act, the Louisiana Purchase, and other policies of Thomas Jefferson so angered his party that he was forced to resign his Senate seat. He accepted the post of minister to Russia in 1809, and while in Europe helped to draw up the Treaty of Ghent. He served as Secretary of State under Monroe, and although the Monroe Doctrine bore the President's name, it was primarily the work of Adams. With three others, he was a candidate for the presidency in 1824. Henry Clay, one of the rival candidates, was instrumental in winning a House of Representatives election victory for Adams. But the narrow margin of support plagued Adams throughout his administration. Defeated for re-election in 1828, he returned to private life but resumed political activity not long afterward as a member of the House of Representatives. A bitter foe of slavery, he attacked a House rule which forbade the discussion of antislavery petitions and succeeded in having it abolished. His journal, a valuable historical document covering more than 60 years, was published in part in 1874–77 in twelve volumes under the title, *Memoirs of John Quincy Adams.*

HENRY CLAY, statesman, was born in Hanover County, Va., April 12, 1777, and died in Washington, D.C., June 29, 1852. As a young clerk in the Virginia High Court of Chancellery he read widely to overcome his deficiencies in formal education, for he had had only three years of schooling. He also studied law under Robert Brooke, Virginia's attorney-general. In 1797 he was licensed to practice and moved to Lexington, Ky. His election to the Kentucky legislature in 1803 started his career as a statesman and orator. In the following years he shuttled between seats in the United States Senate and the legislature until, in 1811, he was elected to the United States House of Representatives. As House Speaker, he advocated the War of 1812 and—later in his Congressional career—tariff protection, a rechartering of the banks, and the Missouri Compromise. In 1814 he resigned from Congress to act as negotiator for the Treaty of Ghent, but he returned to the House the following year. He was defeated for the presidency in a close contest in the House of Representatives. Fourth in electoral votes, he had to cast his own ballot for one of his rivals. Despite instructions from Kentucky to vote for Andrew Jackson, Clay balloted for John Quincy Adams. Jackson's supporters were bitter when Adams later appointed Clay Secretary of State. As a United States Senator, Clay in 1831 became leader of the new Whig party. In the political struggle that followed he was twice more defeated for the presidency, first by his old opponent, Andrew Jackson, and then by James K. Polk. He supported Benjamin Harrison, his own party's candidate, after Harrison won the nomination from him. Once more a senator in 1849, he again steered the country away from open conflict over slavery, this time in the new territory acquired in the Mexican War.

That patriotism which, catching its inspiration from the immortal God, animates and prompts to deeds of self-sacrifice, of valor, of devotion, and of death itself,— that is public virtue, that is the sublimest of all public virtues.

Henry Clay

[ELECTED IN 1900 BY 74 VOTES]

BUST by Robert Aitken; unveiled May 9, 1929; gift of a group of Kentuckians [chiefly through the efforts of Col. Joseph M. Hartfield]; unveiled by Mrs. William Sawitzky, great-granddaughter of the statesman; address by Hon. A. O. Stanley, former U.S. Senator from Kentucky.

Let us look for guidance to the principles of true Democracy, which are enduring because they are right, and invincible because they are just.

Grover Cleveland

[ELECTED IN 1935 BY 77 VOTES]

BUST by Rudulph Evans; unveiled March 18, 1937; gift of many admirers of President Cleveland; formal presentation and the reading of a letter from the President of the United States, Franklin D. Roosevelt, by Dr. John H. Finley; unveiled by Master Thomas Grover Cleveland, grandson of President Cleveland; tribute by Hon. Robert Lincoln O'Brien, Chairman, United States Tariff Commission and former Secretary to President Cleveland, and address by Dr. John Steward Bryan, President, College of William and Mary.

GROVER CLEVELAND, twenty-second and twenty-fourth President of the United States, was born at Caldwell, N.J., March 18, 1837, and died at Princeton, N.J., June 24, 1908. When he was a boy his family moved to Fayetteville, N.Y., and he received his early education at the local academy. The family's limited finances made it impossible for him to study at a law school, but he managed to obtain a clerkship in a Buffalo law office. Here, between clerical chores, he was able to pursue his legal studies. He was admitted to the bar in 1859. His first public office was that of assistant district attorney of Erie County, Buffalo, in 1863. In 1881 he was elected mayor of Buffalo and in 1883, governor of New York. In this office, he showed himself to be an enemy of machine politics. In 1885 he became President, the first Democrat to hold that office after the Civil War. His advocacy of a lower tariff, an issue which dominated the campaign of 1888, probably was responsible for his failure to win re-election that year. He lost the electoral vote to Benjamin Harrison, the Republican candidate, in spite of having received a popular majority. However, he was again elected President in 1892. During his incumbency he promoted nonpartisan civil service, made vigorous attacks on the tariff system by introducing a measure known as the Mills Bill, opposed currency inflation, and brought about the repeal of the silver legislation. A severe depression and labor troubles racked his administration, but he refused to interfere in business matters and rejected as wild theory Jacob Coxey's demand for work relief of $20,000,000 monthly. In 1894, he used troops to move the mail during a Pullman strike. Upon expiration of his second term, he went to Princeton to live in retirement.

BENJAMIN FRANKLIN, statesman, printer, and scientist, was born in Boston, January 17, 1706, and died in Philadelphia, April 17, 1790. The son of a candlemaker, Franklin was apprenticed at the age of 13 to his half brother in the printing trade. After a quarrel over some controversial articles Benjamin had written for the paper, he left for Philadelphia where he was able, after many years, to buy and edit *The Pennsylvania Gazette,* a weekly newspaper. *Poor Richard's Almanack* brought him into the public eye. His accomplishments during this period were many and diverse. In addition to his writings, he established one of the earliest circulating libraries in America, helped found the American Philosophical Society, established an academy which later became the University of Pennsylvania, and was a leading figure in many public reforms. He grew interested in science, and his series of experiments with electricity gained him an international reputation. He also invented bifocal glasses and the harmonica. Popular in England and on the Continent, Franklin at first urged a moderate course on the colonists in their differences with the British, particularly in the matter of the Stamp Act. He had worked for the British cause during the French and Indian War, and his son, William, was to become the leader of the loyalists in the colonies. But in 1775 Franklin came back to America to aid the Revolution, becoming a delegate to the Continental Congress and a member of the committee which drafted and signed the Declaration of Independence. Sent back to Europe, he helped direct American naval operations there, steered United States relations in France, and, in 1781, helped negotiate the peace treaty with Great Britain. At the 1787 convention, he was a powerful force in bringing the United States Constitution into being.

This Constitution can end in despotism, as other forms have done before it, only when the people shall become so corrupted as to need despotic government, being incapable of any other.

Benjamin Franklin

[ELECTED IN 1900 BY 94 VOTES]

BUST by Robert Aitken; unveiled May 5, 1927; gift of the Pennsylvania Society of New York; presented by Colonel Robert Mazet, Secretary of the Society; unveiled by General Hugh L. Scott, great-great-great-grandson of Franklin and formerly Chief of Staff, U.S.A. [Ret.]. Letters read from President Coolidge and His Excellency Monsieur Paul Claudel, Ambassador of the French Republic.

The establishment of a constitution in time of profound peace by the voluntary consent of a whole people is a prodigy to the completion of which I look forward with trembling anxiety.

Alexander Hamilton

[ELECTED IN 1915 BY 70 VOTES]

BUST by Giuseppe Ceracchi; replica unveiled May 22, 1923; gift of the Alexander Hamilton Institute of New York; unveiled by Miss Mary Schuyler Hamilton, greatgranddaughter of Hamilton; address by Dr. Talcott Williams.

ALEXANDER HAMILTON, statesman, was born at Charles Town, Nevis, B.W.I., January 11, 1757, and died in New York City, July 12, 1804. Because of his family's domestic difficulties, he had to earn his own living at the age of 12. In 1772 he came to the American Colonies and two years later, as a student at King's College (now Columbia University), was the author of fiery speeches and pamphlets supporting the cause of the Revolution. During the Revolutionary War he was a captain of artillery, and in this capacity attracted the attention of George Washington by his military skill and daring. He became Washington's aide-de-camp and confidential secretary but resigned the post to take an active part in the fighting at Yorktown. After the war he practiced law in New York. During this period, he completed an outline of a plan for a new government with more central authority than that exercised by the Continental Congress. He propounded these views eloquently as a delegate to the Federal Constitutional Convention. Later, as the nation's first Secretary of the Treasury under George Washington, he had an opportunity to put many of his ideas into practice. In an effort to put the federal government's finances on a firm footing, he proposed that the United States take over state debts, that it raise excise taxes and set up protective tariffs, and that it establish a national bank and a mint. Despite bitter opposition from the Jeffersonians, he succeeded in establishing the bank and in having state debts assumed by the federal government. In 1800 he supported for President his old political opponent, Jefferson, against Aaron Burr, whom he distrusted. Four years later, he again thwarted Burr, who was seeking the New York governorship. Burr challenged Hamilton to a duel and mortally wounded him.

PATRICK HENRY, statesman and orator, was born in Hanover County, Va., May 29, 1736, and died in Charlotte County, Va., June 6, 1799. After a meager education and a succession of business failures, he read enough law to receive a license to practice. His initial recognition as an orator rests on his impassioned plea in "The Parsons' Cause." In that oration, he assailed the King for annulling a Virginia burgesses' statute relating to the payment of clergymen. His stand made him an instant hero among the common people. In May, 1765, he became a member of the Virginia House of Burgesses. Plunged into the debate on the Stamp Act, he delivered his famous speech which evoked cries of "Treason!" and brought his immortal retort: "If this be treason, make the most of it." This made him a rallying point for the cause of independence. He represented Virginia at the first Colonial Congress at Philadelphia on September 5, 1774. As a member of the second Virginia convention at Richmond in March, 1775, he again rose to oratorical heights with his ringing speech that ended: ". . . give me liberty, or give me death!" On August, 5, 1775, he was made commander in chief of Virginia's troops but ended his military service six months later because of what he considered to be interference with his powers. In the 1776 Virginia convention he served on the committee that drafted the first constitution for Virginia. He also was elected governor in each of three successive years. In that office he supported Washington and sent George Rogers Clark with an expedition to harass the British in the Northwest. In 1784 he became governor for the fourth time. He opposed federal government on the grounds that it was dangerous to states' rights. From 1794 until his death he declined offers of higher public office.

Give me liberty or give me death.

Patrick Henry

[ELECTED IN 1920 BY 57 VOTES]

BUST by Charles Keck; unveiled May 8, 1930; gift of Frederic W. Scott of Richmond, Va.; unveiled by Mrs. Henry Sampson, great-granddaughter of the patriot; address by Hon. John Garland Pollard, Governor of Virginia.

Our Federal Union! It must and shall be preserved.

Andrew Jackson

[ELECTED IN 1910 BY 53 VOTES]

Bust by Belle Kinney; unveiled May 13, 1924; gift of the Ladies' Hermitage Association of Nashville, Tenn.; unveiled by Albert Marble Jackson, great-grandson of the President; address by Hon. Norman H. Davis, former Acting Secretary of State.

ANDREW JACKSON, seventh President of the United States, was born in Waxhaw Settlement, S.C., March 15, 1767, and died at "The Hermitage" near Nashville, Tenn., June 8, 1845. His father died shortly before he was born, and the Revolutionary War broke out while he was still a child. He and an older brother skirmished with the British at Hanging Rock, and the following year he and another brother were captured by the British. His mother finally arranged for their exchange, but not before both had caught smallpox from which Andrew's brother died. Soon afterward, his mother died from a fever contracted while she was nursing the sick at Charlestown. Thus orphaned by the war, Andrew nursed a hatred of the British for the remainder of his life. He studied law and moved westward to Nashville, Tenn., where his impetuosity and hot temper kept him embroiled in brawls and duels. Unwittingly, he married Rachel Robard before her divorce proceedings had been completed. Throughout his political career, his enemies used that episode as a weapon against him. He served in the United States House of Representatives, the United States Senate, and as judge of the Tennessee Superior Court. During the War of 1812 he won the rank of major general. His inspiring postwar victory over the British at New Orleans made him a national hero and paved his way to the presidency. Known as a champion of his soldiers, frontiersmen, and the common people generally, he was fondly referred to as "Old Hickory." At one point, he exceeded his authority by marching his troops into Spanish Florida on a punitive expedition against the Indians; the incident brought the country to the brink of war with Spain and England, but Jackson's popularity only increased. He gained the Presidency easily in 1828 and served two terms.

THOMAS JEFFERSON, third President of the United States, was born at Shadwell, Va., April 13, 1743, and died at Monticello, Va., July 4, 1826. He was graduated from William and Mary in 1762 and studied law under the scholar, George Wythe. While serving in the House of Burgesses, Jefferson wrote a paper, *A Summary View of the Rights of British America,* in which he declared that the colonists' sole tie to England was their allegiance to the King. Parliament, he said, had no authority in colonial matters. While serving in the Continental Congress of 1775–76 he was appointed to draft the Declaration of Independence. During the Revolution he was governor of Virginia when it was invaded by the British. In 1783 he again served in the Continental Congress and later became minister to France. He returned home after a futile attempt to negotiate a trade treaty with England. He became Washington's Secretary of State in 1790. Jefferson was an advocate of universal education, religious freedom, and state administration of local matters. Upon returning from England, he first came into serious conflict with Federalism and its leader, Alexander Hamilton. Quarrels with Hamilton finally led Jefferson to leave his cabinet post in 1793. A new political party (called the Republican but actually the forerunner of today's Democratic party) formed around him and supported him for the presidency in 1800. When he and Aaron Burr tied in the voting, the contest went to the House of Representatives for a decision. Only after his old opponent, Hamilton, who distrusted Burr, had thrown his support to Jefferson on the 36th ballot was the presidency decided. Jefferson served two terms. His greatest single achievement was the purchase of Louisiana from France and his dispatching of the Lewis and Clark expedition.

We hold these truths to be self-evident: that all men are created equal; that they are endowed by their Creator with certain inalienable rights; that among these are life, liberty and the pursuit of happiness.

Thomas Jefferson

[ELECTED IN 1900 BY 91 VOTES]

BUST by Robert Aitken; unveiled May 13, 1924; gift of the Jefferson Boys' Pilgrimage Committee and others, through the New York World; unveiled by Mrs. Francis O. Barton, great-great-granddaughter of President Jefferson; address by Dr. Edwin A. Alderman, President of the University of Virginia.

With malice towards none, with charity for all, with firmness in the right as God gives us to see the right, let us strive on to finish the work we are in.

Abraham Lincoln

[ELECTED IN 1900 BY 96 VOTES]

BUST by Augustus Saint-Gaudens; replica unveiled May 22, 1923; gift of the Union League Club of Chicago; unveiled by Mrs. Mary Lincoln Isham, granddaughter of Lincoln; address by His Excellency Monsieur J. J. Jusserand, Ambassador of the French Republic.

ABRAHAM LINCOLN, sixteenth President of the United States, was born in Hardin County, Ky., February 12, 1809, and died in Washington, D.C., April 15, 1865. The son of a frontiersman, he worked at heavy labor all day and read at night to make up for his lack of schooling. His mother died when he was a youth and his father remarried. Lincoln's stepmother encouraged the boy's interest in books. Defeated in his first campaign for an Illinois legislative seat, he was elected four times between 1834 and 1840. During this period he was licensed as an attorney and went to Springfield to practice. Here he married Mary Todd in 1842. He first held national office in 1846 upon election to Congress as a Whig. He began to attract wide attention with his debates with Douglas over the slavery question. Despite the powerful "house divided" speech with which Lincoln opened his 1858 senatorial campaign against Douglas, the latter won re-election. But two years later, Lincoln was elected President as a Republican. He never wavered in his determination to save the Union. Fort Sumter was fired on in April, 1861, plunging the nation into civil war. The early war years were filled with dissension in Lincoln's cabinet, criticism of his policies, and military defeat. He seized upon the Union victory at Antietam as an opportunity for issuing the Emancipation Proclamation of September 22, 1862. But his most famous address was delivered at the dedication of the military cemetery at Gettysburg, Pa. With victory near, Lincoln later voiced his hope for reconciliation between the North and South. He did not live to put his reconstruction policy into action. He was assassinated at Ford's Theater by John Wilkes Booth.

JAMES MADISON, fourth President of the United States, was born at Port Conway, Va., March 16, 1751, and died at Montpelier, Va., June 28, 1836. After being graduated from Princeton, he studied philosophy, theology, and law. In 1776 he helped to draft the constitution for the new state of Virginia. During the early days of the republic he served in the Continental Congress and in the Virginia legislature. Madison was a staunch proponent of the 1787 convention at which he helped to draft the federal Constitution. He was also a strong advocate of the Bill of Rights and later, in Virginia, led the forces that urged its adoption. Moreover, he joined Alexander Hamilton and John Jay in writing the *Federalist* in an effort to overcome objections to the Constitution. He was a strong supporter of Jefferson, and when the latter became President in 1801, Madison became his Secretary of State and served during both of Jefferson's terms. In that capacity, Madison played a major role in the Louisiana Purchase. In 1809 Madison was elected President and served two terms. The War of 1812 was opposed bitterly by the industrialists and merchants of New England, who considered the hostilities a blow to commerce. During the early days of the war, many talked of rebelling rather than pursuing what they called "Mr. Madison's War." The fortunes of the United States reached their lowest point in 1814 when the British captured Washington and burned the White House. Madison's wife, Dolly, is credited with saving historic documents, portraits, and other valuable objects at that crucial point. The Treaty of Ghent ended the war and lifted the gloom which darkened Madison's presidential terms. He remained in office long enough to see the beginning of America's feverish westward expansion to the Pacific.

Governments do better without kings and nobles than with them; religion flourishes in greater purity without than with the aid of government.

James Madison

[ELECTED IN 1905 BY 56 VOTES]

BUST by Charles Keck; unveiled May 9, 1929; gift of the General Society of Princeton Alumni [of which Madison was the founder]; unveiled by Miss Betty Glenn Walker, a descendant of Madison's brother; address by Dr. Thomas J. Wertenbaker, representing Dr. John Grier Hibben, President of Princeton University.

The cause of liberty . . . animated my youthful days; it has engaged the zealous attention of my maturer years; it will command my best efforts in its support so long as I shall be permitted to live.

James Monroe

[ELECTED IN 1930 BY 66 VOTES]

BUST by Hermon A. MacNeil; unveiled May 14, 1931; gift of the James Monroe High School; presented by the Principal of the High School, Dr. Henry E. Hein; unveiled by Mrs. Rose Gouverneur Hoes, great-granddaughter of Monroe; address by Hon. Henry Morgenthau, former Ambassador to Turkey. A letter from the President of the United States, Herbert Hoover, was read, and a letter on the Monroe Doctrine by Hon. Elihu Root, former Secretary of State, was also read by Dr. John H. Finley.

JAMES MONROE, fifth President of the United States, was born in Westmoreland County, Va., April 28, 1758, and died in New York City, July 4, 1831. The Revolutionary War broke out while he was a student at William and Mary, and he left his studies to fight. But in 1780 he withdrew from military service to study law under Thomas Jefferson; the step marked the beginning of a lifelong friendship. In 1782 he was elected to the Virginia legislature, and from 1783 to 1786 was in the Congress of the Confederation. At the Federal Constitutional Convention he joined Patrick Henry in opposing certain features of the Constitution. Later, in the United States Senate, he was an outspoken supporter of Jefferson in the latter's skirmishes with Hamilton and the Federalists. Appointed minister to France, Monroe was recalled in 1796 as a consequence of a particularly bitter attack by Federalists on Jeffersonian policy. At the turn of the century he served as governor of Virginia. When the election of 1800 restored the power of the Jeffersonians, Monroe again was sent to France, this time as a special envoy. Among other things, he helped Robert R. Livingston, the resident minister, to negotiate the Louisiana Purchase. Monroe again served as governor of Virginia upon returning to America and was then made Secretary of State under Madison. For a time, he also acted as Secretary of War; he filled both posts with diligence and energy. He was elected President as a Republican in 1816 and was re-elected in 1820. Perhaps the most lasting accomplishment of his second term was his enunciation of the Monroe Doctrine, drafted primarily by his Secretary of State, John Quincy Adams. It stemmed from Russian attempts to colonize the Pacific Northwest and from the Holy Alliance's plans to return Latin America to colonial status.

WILLIAM PENN, statesman and founder of Pennsylvania, was born in London, October 14, 1644, and died at Ruscombe, England, July 30, 1718. The son of Sir William Penn, an influential British admiral, he underwent at the age of 11 a profound religious awakening that shaped his entire life. At the age of 18 he proclaimed himself a Quaker, but he drifted away from the sect during a period spent on the Continent. Sent to Ireland in 1666 to manage his father's estates, he returned to Quakerism and never again deserted it. He entered upon a life of preaching and writing in advocacy of freedom of conscience and was jailed repeatedly as a result. He carried his campaign to Germany and the Netherlands and—after 1675—to America. In that year he acquired title to western New Jersey lands which he opened to persecuted Quakers. The project prospered; and in 1681, in payment of a debt owed his father, he received a great tract of land from Charles II under the name "Pennsilvania." He also received a charter which gave him broad governmental powers. The right of petition, trial by jury, provisions for annual elections, and the guarantee of freedom of worship were basic elements of the new government. It wasn't until October 27, 1682, that Penn stepped ashore in America. He landed at New Castle, in the present state of Delaware, which the Duke of York had ceded to him. He continued on to Philadelphia, already the scene of building activity. His fairness in dealing with the Indians won their friendship. He remained two years before returning to London, where political harassment, arrests, and imprisonment kept him from returning to America until 1699. The colony prospered until he sailed for England in 1701, never to return. Political and financial difficulties plagued him for the next ten years.

Governments, like clocks, go from the motion men give them; and as governments are made and moved by men, so by them they are ruined too. . . . Governments rather depend upon men, than men upon governments . . . if men be bad, let the government be never so good, they will endeavor to warp and spoil it to their turn.

William Penn

[ELECTED IN 1935 BY 83 VOTES]

BUST by A. Stirling Calder; unveiled May 28, 1936; gift of The Genealogical Society of Pennsylvania, and The Associate Committee of Women, The Historical Society of Pennsylvania, The Welcome Society of Pennsylvania, Friends' Historical Association, The Pennsylvania Society of the Colonial Dames of America, and many other organizations; presented by Dr. William Wistar Comfort, President of Haverford College; unveiled by Philip Penn-Gaskell Hall, Jr., ninth in descent from William Penn; address by His Excellency George H. Earle, Governor of Pennsylvania.

That man is the best American who has in him the American spirit, the American soul. Such a man fears not the strong and harms not the weak. He scorns what is base or cruel or dishonest. He looks beyond the accidents of occupation or social condition and hails each of his fellow citizens as his brother.

Theodore Roosevelt

[ELECTED IN 1950 BY 70 VOTES]

Bust by Georg Lober; unveiled May 9, 1954; gift of the Theodore Roosevelt Association; formal presentation by Mr. Oscar S. Straus II, President of the Theodore Roosevelt Association; unveiled by Mrs. Nicholas Longworth, daughter of Theodore Roosevelt; tribute by Mr. Hermann Hagedorn, Director, Theodore Roosevelt Association. The principal address was delivered by Hon. Harold E. Stassen, Director, Foreign Operations Administration. Music for the ceremony by Thomas L. Thomas and the New York University Glee Club.

THEODORE ROOSEVELT, twenty-sixth President of the United States, was born in New York City, October 27, 1858, and died at Oyster Bay, L.I., N.Y., January 6, 1919. A Phi Beta Kappa graduate of Harvard, he was in the New York State Assembly from 1882 to 1884, ran unsuccessfully for governor in 1886, and was appointed Civil Service commissioner by President Harrison in 1888. Continuing his political career, he became president of the board of police commissioners in New York, assistant secretary of the Navy under President McKinley, and governor of New York. He was elected Vice-President in 1900 and became President when McKinley was assassinated a year later; in 1904 he was elected to a full term. His administrations were marked by the aftermath of the Spanish-American War, which had made him a popular hero as a result of his role in recruiting Colonel Leonard Wood's Rough Riders. With the military backing of the Roosevelt administration, Panama seceded from Colombia, paving the way for the United States to build the Isthmian canal. As Roosevelt put it: "I took the Canal Zone and let Congress debate, and while the debate goes on the Canal does also." This action and other unilateral Roosevelt moves in the Caribbean evoked strong and long-lasting resentment among Latin Americans. Meanwhile, in the Orient, Roosevelt sought to negotiate an open-door policy with China and mediated the end of the Russo-Japanese war. In 1906 he was awarded the Nobel Peace Prize. Domestically, he fought corruption and business trusts, intervened on the public's behalf in a 1902 coal strike, and was an ardent supporter of conservation. A stout friend of England, he opposed American neutrality in the First World War. He was a rugged outdoorsman and also a prolific writer.

GEORGE WASHINGTON, first President of the United States, was born near Fredericksburg, Westmoreland County, Va., February 22, 1732, and died at Mount Vernon, Va., December 14, 1799. As a youth he helped survey northern Virginia and Shenandoah Valley lands belonging to the Fairfax family. When his half brother, Lawrence, went to Barbados to recover his failing health, Washington went along. Here he contracted smallpox, thus becoming immune to the disease which later was to ravage his troops. His stepbrother died after returning to the Colonies, and George was named executor of the estate; he managed its affairs for the next two decades. He also received the post of district military adjutant with the rank of major. After taking part in the closing battles of the French and Indian Wars, he became a member of the House of Burgesses; here he voiced opposition to British colonial policies. He emerged into national life as a member of the Continental Congress in 1774–75 and, with John Adams' help, was named commander in chief of the Continental forces. He took command at Cambridge, Mass., on July 3, 1775. His first victory was the occupation of Dorchester Heights, a maneuver that forced the British out of Boston. But defeats followed, culminating in the winter at Valley Forge. However, spring brought reinforcements and increased powers from Congress. For the colonials, victory followed victory. Defeated, Cornwallis surrendered to Washington at Yorktown, Va., October 19, 1781. After the war, Washington helped to bring about ratification of the Constitution. He was unanimously chosen first President of the United States and took office in New York on April 30, 1789. He served two terms but refused a third. Honored and revered as "the father of his country," he retired to his estate at Mount Vernon.

Promote, then, as an object of primary importance, institutions for the general diffusion of knowledge. Of all the dispositions and habits which lead to political prosperity, religion and morality are indispensable supports. Reason and experience both forbid us to expect that national morality can prevail in exclusion of religious principles.

George Washington

[ELECTED IN 1900 BY 97 VOTES]

BUST by Jean-Antoine Houdon; replica unveiled May 20, 1922; gift of the New York City Chapter of the Daughters of the American Revolution; unveiled by Field-Marshal Earl French of Ypres; address by Dr. John H. Finley.

I profess, in my career hitherto, to have kept steadily in view the prosperity and honor of the whole country and the preservation of our Federal Union.

Daniel Webster

[ELECTED IN 1900 BY 96 VOTES]

BUST by Robert Aitken; unveiled May 12, 1926; gift of the New Hampshire Historical Society; unveiled by Samuel A. Appleton, great-grandson of Webster; address by Hon. George W. Wickersham, former Attorney-General of the United States.

DANIEL WEBSTER, statesman, was born in Salisbury (now Franklin), N.H., January 18, 1782, and died in Marshfield, Mass., October 24, 1852. Graduated from Dartmouth in 1801, he was admitted to the bar in Boston in 1805 and set up practice in Portsmouth, N.H. He rose rapidly in law and politics. At the beginning of the War of 1812 he opposed the Madison administration and was elected to the United States House of Representatives by the Federalists. Henry Clay, the House Speaker, named Webster to the Committee on Foreign Relations, of which John C. Calhoun was chairman. For the next 40 years these three were the dominant figures in American politics. Webster won fame for his oratory on the House floor by his eloquent opposition to the conduct of the war. In arguing the Dartmouth College case before the United States Supreme Court, he won not only the case and personal fame but a victory for federal government over states' rights—a principle he advocated all his life. Among his outstanding speeches were orations in 1820 at Plymouth marking the second centennial of the Pilgrims' landing; in 1825 at the Bunker Hill monument cornerstone rites; and in 1826 in commemoration of John Adams and Thomas Jefferson, both of whom died on July 4th of that year. He was Secretary of State briefly under Harrison and Tyler and negotiated the Webster-Ashburton Treaty, removing several dangerous points of friction with Britain. In the growing quarrel between North and South, he made his last great speech, "The Seventh of March Speech," supporting Clay's compromise of 1850. It was Webster's effort to win lasting settlement of the slavery question, but many Northerners regarded it as a betrayal. He was again Secretary of State in Fillmore's cabinet.

WOODROW WILSON, twenty-eighth President of the United States, was born at Staunton, Va., December 28, 1856, and died in Washington, D.C., February 3, 1924. By the time he was graduated from the College of New Jersey (now Princeton), he already had decided on a public career. He then studied law at the University of Virginia, practiced briefly, and obtained a doctorate at Johns Hopkins in 1886. At the age of 34 he became professor of jurisprudence and political economy at Princeton and assumed the university presidency two years later in 1902. He won wide recognition by introducing the preceptorial system at Princeton. His attempts to introduce other reforms there were blocked by influential alumni; nevertheless, they earned him the New Jersey gubernatorial nomination, and he was elected in 1910. After disavowing any help from Tammany, he was elected President in 1912. His reforms included the Underwood tariff, the Federal Reserve Act, creation of the Federal Trade Commission, and the Clayton Antitrust Act. With the nation seething over the sinking of the "Lusitania," Wilson was re-elected in 1916 on his pledge to keep out of war "if it is possible." Only after repeated provocations, including the sinking of four more American ships, did he ask Congress to declare war on Germany in April, 1917. In January, 1918, he outlined in Congress his "Fourteen Points," which later were used in negotiating peace. At the Versailles peace talks, he strongly advocated a League of Nations, but opposition in the United States Senate was formidable. Wilson toured the United States on behalf of the League. However, at Pueblo, Colo., he suffered a stroke which incapacitated him. The Versailles treaty was rejected by the Senate. Nevertheless, Wilson won the Nobel Peace Prize in 1919.

The interests of all nations are our own also. We are partners with the rest.

What we seek is the reign of law, based upon the consent of the governed and sustained by the organized opinion of mankind.

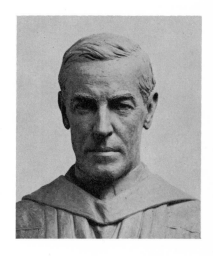

Woodrow Wilson

[ELECTED IN 1950 BY 77 VOTES]

BUST by Walker Kirtland Hancock; unveiled May 20, 1956; gift of The Woodrow Wilson Foundation; formal presentation by Mr. August Heckscher, President of The Woodrow Wilson Foundation; unveiled by Mrs. Woodrow Wilson, widow of President Wilson; address by Mr. Dag Hammarskjold, Secretary-General, United Nations. Music for the ceremony by the New York University Chapel Choir.

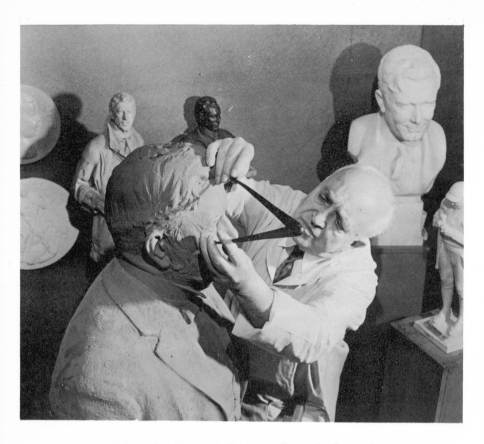

*Edmondo Quattrocchi at work on the bust of
George Westinghouse for the Hall of Fame.*

XIII

BUSINESS MEN AND
PHILANTHROPISTS

PETER COOPER, manufacturer and philanthropist, was born in New York City, February 12, 1791, and died there on April 4, 1883. After early training in various family enterprises, he went into business for himself. His future fortune was founded on a glue factory which he bought in Manhattan and with which he managed to monopolize the market in American-made glue and isinglass. But the bulk of his fortune came from enterprises relating to the Canton Iron Works, which he and two partners established in Baltimore in 1828. Here was built "Tom Thumb," the first locomotive constructed in the United States. Built especially to travel along the twisting, steep-graded tracks of the Baltimore and Ohio Railroad, it could pull 40 persons at ten miles an hour. It was instrumental in keeping the financially distressed railroad in operation. Cooper's holdings grew rapidly to include railway stock, blast furnaces, a wire manufacturing plant, iron mines, foundries, and a rolling mill. One of his products, the first iron structured specifically for fireproof buildings, helped to win him the Bessemer Gold Medal, awarded by the Iron and Steel Institute of Great Britain. As president of the North American Telegraph Company and the New York, Newfoundland, and London Telegraph Company, Cooper was a long-time supporter of Cyrus Field and his plan to lay the Atlantic cable. Cooper also was an inventor whose devices included propulsion mechanisms for ferryboats and barges as well as a washing machine. As a New York City alderman, he was an early advocate of paid police and fire departments and public schools. He is chiefly remembered as the founder of Cooper Union in New York City, an institute which provides free courses in science, engineering, and the arts.

The great object I desire to accomplish is to open the avenue of scientific knowledge to youth [and so unfold the volume of nature], so that the young may see the beauties of Creation, enjoy its blessings, and learn to love the Author.

Peter Cooper

[ELECTED IN 1900 BY 69 VOTES]

BUST by Chester Beach; unveiled May 13, 1924; gift of Graduates of Cooper Union; unveiled by Miss Edith Cram, great-great-granddaughter of Cooper; address by R. Fulton Cutting, President of Cooper Union.

Looking forward beyond my stay on earth I see our country becoming richer and more powerful. But to make her prosperity more than superficial, her moral and intellectual development should keep pace with her material growth.

George Peabody

[ELECTED IN 1900 BY 74 VOTES]

BUST by Hans Schuler; unveiled May 12, 1926; gift of the Peabody Institute of Baltimore, and of friends and relatives of Peabody; unveiled by Dr. Murray Peabody Brush, great-nephew of Peabody; address by Dr. Bruce R. Payne, President of the George Peabody College of Nashville.

GEORGE PEABODY, merchant, financier, and philanthropist, was born in South Danvers (now Peabody), Mass., February 18, 1795, and died in London, November 4, 1869. At 11 he was apprenticed to a grocer and, through successive promotions, had become by 1814 a partner in a wholesale drygoods warehouse. From Baltimore he often made business trips to England. There in 1835 he negotiated an $8,000,000 loan for the financially distressed state of Maryland. For this first great public service he received the legislature's vote of thanks. After he had incorporated and built the Eastern Railroad, he settled permanently in London where he headed a firm specializing in foreign exchange and American securities. He soon became the prototype of the rich, generous American. While he usually ignored direct appeals for charity, he gave $15,000 to display American products and inventions in London's Crystal Palace after Congress had refused to vote funds. Enormously successful in business, he did much to restore America's shaken credit standing abroad. He gave $10,000 to fit out a ship in order to search for Sir John Franklin, the Arctic explorer. Peabody's Fourth of July dinner parties in London were memorable events, and did much to cement Anglo-American relations. His gifts to United States education included the Peabody Institute, Baltimore, which provided a library, lecture endowment, academy of music, and art gallery. He also endowed the Peabody Institute at Peabody, Mass.; the Peabody Museum of natural history at Yale; the Peabody Museum of archaeology and ethnology at Harvard; the Peabody Academy of Science at Salem, Mass., and the $3,500,000 Peabody Education Fund for the promotion of education in the South. England's tributes to Peabody were many, including burial in Westminster Abbey.

XIV

ARTISTS

EDWIN BOOTH, actor, was born near Bel Air, Md., November 13, 1833, and died in New York, June 7, 1893. Reared in the theatrical tradition (his father, Junius Brutus Booth, was a stage favorite in both England and America), Booth made his stage debut at the Boston Museum as Tressel to his father's Richard III on September 10, 1849. Two years later in New York, his erratic father without warning one night forced the son to go on stage as Richard III. After his father's death in 1852, Booth played performances in California, Australia, Hawaii, and Europe. In 1863 he became manager of the Winter Garden Theater in New York and there presented Shakespeare on a scale unprecedented in polish and grandeur. He and his brothers, Junius Brutus, Jr. and John Wilkes Booth, respectively, played Brutus, Cassius, and Mark Antony in an outstanding presentation of *Julius Caesar*. Between November 26, 1864, and March 22, 1865, Edwin played Hamlet for 100 consecutive nights. At the height of this triumph he was forced into retirement by public reaction to his brother's assassination of President Lincoln in April. But early in 1866 Edwin returned to resume the role of Hamlet at the Winter Garden. Later, he built his own million-dollar New York theater, which opened in 1869 with *Romeo and Juliet*. There he produced Shakespeare and other plays of uniformly high quality for five years before the financial panic of 1873–74 forced him into bankruptcy and cost him his theater. However, he later recouped his fortune. Between 1880 and 1883 he revisited Europe, winning acclaim in England, Germany, and Austria. His last appearance was as Hamlet, which generally is conceded to have been his finest role, at the Brooklyn Academy of Music in 1891. In 1888 he founded and was first president of The Players club in New York.

Hamlet was the epitome of mankind, not an individual, a sort of magic mirror in which all men and women see the reflex of themselves.

Edwin Booth

[ELECTED IN 1925 BY 85 VOTES]

BUST by Edmond T. Quinn; unveiled May 12, 1926; gift of The Players; unveiled by Edwin Booth Grossman, grandson of Booth; address by Augustus Thomas, playwright and member of the American Academy of Arts and Letters.

To be thoroughly in earnest, intensely in earnest in all my thoughts and in all my actions, whether in my profession or out of it, became my one single idea.

Charlotte Saunders Cushman

[ELECTED IN 1915 BY 53 VOTES]

BUST by Francis Grimes; unveiled May 21, 1925; gift of men and women of the stage and admirers and relatives of Miss Cushman; unveiled by Dr. Allerton S. Cushman, great-nephew of Miss Cushman; address by Otis Skinner.

CHARLOTTE SAUNDERS CUSHMAN, actress, was born in Boston, Mass., July 23, 1816, and died there February 17, 1876. She made her debut as an opera singer in *The Marriage of Figaro* at the Tremont Theater in Boston. With the company, she went to New Orleans where—either because of a personal whim or because her deep voice had been strained in soprano roles—she gave up opera for acting. At the age of 19 she made her first appearance in a dramatic role as Lady Macbeth. She then went to New York to play an engagement at the Bowery Theater. During the play's run the theater burned, along with most of her wardrobe. While the theater was being rebuilt she went to Albany, where she played Romeo and Belvidera, the latter in the play *Venice Preserved*. Back in New York City she was praised by critics for her role of Meg Merrilies in the play *Guy Mannering*, and for her Nancy Sykes in *Oliver Twist*. After two years as stage manager at the Walnut Street Theater in Philadelphia, she determined to conquer the London stage. In 1845 she began a series of triumphs there: Bianca, in support of Edwin Forrest, in *Fazio*; Lady Macbeth, Rosalind, and Romeo to her sister's Juliet. In 1849 she returned to America where she was proclaimed the country's leading actress. She soon earned a fortune and announced her retirement. She moved to London but returned several years later. Again and again she announced her retirement, only to return for a series of brilliant performances, both in the United States and abroad. Her last appearance on any stage was at Eaton, Pa., on June 2, 1875. During her 40 years on the stage critics praised her strong, magnetic, deep-voiced interpretations, her "liberated power, passionate feeling, poetic magnificence, and dramatic effect." She had, one critic wrote, "the attributes of genius."

STEPHEN COLLINS FOSTER, composer, was born in Pittsburgh, Pa., July 4, 1826, and died in New York City, January 13, 1864. His first known composition was "The Tioga Waltz," for flute ensemble; it dates from about 1840. While his father, a well-to-do Pittsburgh merchant, recognized that his son had a "strange talent," he did not feel it necessary to provide a musical education. Stephen's fine ear and sense of rhythm found expression through membership in the Thespian Society, which put on minstrel shows in Pittsburgh. His formal education was scanty; he spent two years at Athens Academy and an apathetic few months at Jefferson College. Later, he was sent to his brother's office in Cincinnati as a bookkeeper, but the publication of his songs allowed him to quit his job after four years and live on his earnings. His first published song, "Open the Lattice, Love," appeared in 1842. It was followed by a long list of others, including "The Old Folks at Home," "Massa's in de Cold, Cold Ground," "My Old Kentucky Home," "Old Dog Tray," "Old Black Joe," "Jeanie with the Light Brown Hair," and "Come Where My Love Lies Dreaming." His royalties became enormous; he was said to have received $15,000 for one song alone. Played and sung at home and abroad by the E. P. Cristy minstrel troupe, Foster's songs achieved wide popularity. With the exception of a trip to New Orleans in 1852 and a brief visit to New York in 1853, Foster spent most of his life in Pittsburgh. A biographer, H. V. Milligan, says that in Foster's songs, "the Negro ceases to be a caricature and becomes a human being." Foster wrote 175 songs; the last one published was "Beautiful Dreamer" (1864).

Stephen Collins Foster

[ELECTED IN 1940 BY 86 VOTES]

BUST by Walker Kirtland Hancock; unveiled May 27, 1941; gift of Josiah Kirby Lilly, Stephen J. Wigmore, Mrs. Agnetta F. Kerns, Mr. and Mrs. Fletcher Hodges, Jr., and Judson Cole; formal presentation by Josiah Kirby Lilly, Founder of the Foster Hall Collection of the University of Pittsburgh; unveiled by Foster's granddaughter, Mrs. Jessie Welch Rose; tribute by John Tasker Howard, biographer of Foster. An address prepared by Dr. Howard Hanson, Director of the Eastman School of Music, was read in his absence by Dr. Sigmund Spaeth; music by Rose Bampton, Albert Spalding, and New York University Glee Club.

Edward Alexander MacDowell

[ELECTED IN 1960 BY 72 VOTES]

EDWARD ALEXANDER MACDOWELL, composer, was born in New York City, December 18, 1861, and died there, January 23, 1908. The product of a home rich in culture and affection, he studied the piano while attending public school. In 1876 his mother took him to Paris to continue his musical education at the Conservatoire. Later, he studied in Germany. At the age of 20 he was nominated by Carl Heymann, the brilliant pianist, to succeed him on the Frankfort Conservatory faculty. Although rejected by the faculty, the nomination won MacDowell wide recognition in the musical world. He began to take private pupils, including Marian Nevins, whom he married in 1884. In 1882 he called on Liszt at Weimar, taking with him the manuscript of his first concerto in A-minor (opus 15). Impressed, Liszt recommended MacDowell's *First Modern Suite* (opus 10) for the program of the 19th annual convention of the German music confederation in Zurich that summer. MacDowell himself played the suite, which—together with the *Second Modern Suite* (opus 14)—appeared the following year as his first published work. During the period spent near Wiesbaden after his marriage he produced orchestral and piano compositions and songs, including the symphonic poems *Lancelot and Elaine* (opus 25) and *The Lovely Alda* (opus 30). In 1888 he returned to Boston to devote himself to teaching, composing, and giving recitals. *Woodland Sketches* belongs to this period. In 1896 he accepted a music professorship at Columbia University. He spent his summers composing in a log cabin on his farm at Peterboro, N.H. After his death his widow dedicated the estate as a memorial equipped with studios for poets, musicians, painters, and sculptors.

[BUST has not yet been unveiled.]

AUGUSTUS SAINT-GAUDENS, sculptor, was born in Dublin, Ireland, March 1, 1848, and died in Cornish, N.H., August 3, 1907. Brought to New York as an infant, he was apprenticed at the age of 13 to a cameo-cutter and spent several years at that occupation. He also studied drawing at Cooper Union and at the National Academy of Design in New York. Shortly before leaving for Paris in 1867 he completed a bronze bust of his father. After studying in Paris, he went to Rome, where he completed his first full figure, "Hiawatha." This sculpture marked him as an artist of immense skill and originality. He returned to New York in 1873 and began an artistic career that was highly prolific. As a diversion from his larger works, he often posed his friends for medallions and plaques. He won unquestioned recognition as a new leader in art with his statue of Admiral Farragut, commissioned in 1876 for Madison Square in New York. It received lavish praise when it was exhibited in plaster at the Paris salon of 1880, and again when it was unveiled in New York the following year. Among his greatest masterpieces were the statue of Lincoln, unveiled in 1887 in Chicago's Lincoln Park, and the Adams memorial statue (1891) in Rock Creek cemetery, Washington, D.C. This mysterious draped figure, often mistakenly regarded as a personification of grief, was intended to symbolize everlasting rest. Another noteworthy work was his equestrian statue of General Sherman which stands at Fifth Avenue and 59th Street in New York. It received the highest honors when it was displayed at the Paris Exposition of 1900. Saint-Gaudens was made an officer of the Legion of Honor and a corresponding member of the Institute of France. He bequeathed to art not only his own works but an influence that freed American sculpture from sterile convention.

Too much time cannot be spent in a task that is to endure for centuries.

Augustus Saint-Gaudens

[ELECTED IN 1920 BY 67 VOTES]

BUST by James Earle Fraser; unveiled May 12, 1926; gift of the National Sculpture Society; unveiled by the grandchildren of Saint-Gaudens, Augustus and Carlota Saint-Gaudens; address by Herbert Adams, member of the American Academy of Arts and Letters, and former President of the National Sculpture Society.

The portrait of George Washington was undertaken by me. It has been indeed the object of the most valuable years of my life to obtain the portrait.

Gilbert Charles Stuart

[ELECTED IN 1900 BY 52 VOTES]

BUST by Laura Gardin Fraser; unveiled May 20, 1922; gift of many citizens; unveiled, with address, by Miss Cecilia Beaux.

GILBERT CHARLES STUART, painter, was born in Kings (now Washington) County, R.I., December 3, 1755, and died in Boston, July 9, 1828. About 1769 Cosmo Alexander, a Scottish artist, came to Newport where Stuart then lived, and gave lessons to the boy who had shown some talent in sketching. Later, the two sailed to Edinburgh; but when Alexander died shortly thereafter, Stuart was forced to work his way home on a ship. Because there was no opportunity for artists in the Colonies in those pre-Revolutionary days, Stuart went to London in 1775. He made a precarious living as a portraitist and church organist. His prospects brightened when Benjamin West, then a leading English painter, took him in as a pupil and later as a member of his household. Stuart's first showing in a Royal Academy exhibition in 1777 was followed by others. His "Portrait of a Gentleman Skating," exhibited in 1782, established him with the public, and commissions began to flow in. During the remainder of his twelve-year stay in London he rose in popularity until his works commanded prices exceeded by none but Reynolds' and Gainsborough's. In 1787 he moved to Dublin, where his success was repeated. Several years later he returned to the United States, and in 1794 he set up a studio in Philadelphia, then the national capital. Here he painted his first two life portraits of Washington; the third, painted at his Germantown studio, was the familiar "Athenaeum Head," an idealized representation of Washington in his old age. Stuart followed the seat of government to Washington in 1803 and there painted Jefferson, Madison, Monroe, and numerous other national figures. In 1805 he moved to Boston, where he spent the remainder of his life. Here, too, he was overwhelmed by commissions. He painted on despite failing health.

JAMES ABBOTT MCNEILL WHISTLER, painter, was born in Lowell, Mass., July 10, 1834, and died in London, July 17, 1903. As a boy he lived in St. Petersburg, where his father, a military engineer, was directing construction of a railroad for the Czar of Russia. Dismissed from the West Point military academy after three years, the boy was employed briefly as a Coast and Geodetic Survey draftsman and map engraver. Here he doubtless learned techniques that furthered his career as an artist. In 1855 he went to Paris to study art. During this period he shuttled between London and Paris. In 1860 the Royal Academy showed his "At the Piano." To the "French Set" of renderings Whistler added the "Thames Set," etchings of embankment scenes and shipping along the river. In the 1870's he produced his celebrated "Nocturne" series treating nighttime scenes in a distinctive manner. Among these was "Nocturne in Black and Gold: The Falling Rocket"; it drew from Ruskin the contemptuous remark that Whistler was "flinging a pot of paint in the public's face." In the resulting libel suit against Ruskin, Whistler spent more than £300 to win the nominal award of a farthing, which he thereafter wore proudly on his watch chain. His most widely known work was "Mrs. George Washington Whistler" (1872), called "Arrangement in Grey and Black No. 1" by the artist and popularly titled "Whistler's Mother." Financially distressed after the libel suit, Whistler went to Venice, where he resumed his old craft of etching to renew his fortunes. The years following his return to London brought him increasing popularity. From 1886 to 1888 he was president of the Royal Society of British Artists; but when he failed to be reelected in 1889, he became embittered. His last years were marred by increasingly vituperative exchanges with critics.

Nature contains the elements in color and form, of all pictures, as the keyboard contains the notes of all music. But the artist is born to pick, and choose, and group with science, these elements, that the result may be beautiful.

James Abbott McNeill Whistler

[ELECTED IN 1930 BY 74 VOTES]

BUST by Frederick MacMonnies; unveiled May 14, 1931; gift of Clarence H. Mackay, George Dupont Pratt, and others; presented by Charles C. Curran, Secretary of the National Academy of Design; unveiled by Mrs. Joseph Pennell, friend and biographer of Whistler; address by Royal Cortissoz, member of the American Academy of Arts and Letters.

APPENDICES

A portion of the pavilion of Statesmen.

Names Honored in the Hall of Fame for Great Americans

The names to be inscribed in the Hall of Fame are chosen every five years by a College of Electors consisting of approximately one hundred American men and women of distinction representing all sections of the country and several professions. Election to the Hall of Fame requires an affirmative vote of a majority of the entire body of Electors. Following, in order of selection, are the names of the eighty-nine persons honored to date:

1900

John Adams
John James Audubon
Henry Ward Beecher
William Ellery Channing
Henry Clay
Peter Cooper
Jonathan Edwards
Ralph Waldo Emerson
David Glasgow Farragut
Benjamin Franklin
Robert Fulton
Ulysses Simpson Grant
Asa Gray
Nathaniel Hawthorne
Washington Irving
Thomas Jefferson
James Kent
Robert Edward Lee
Abraham Lincoln
Henry Wadsworth Longfellow
Horace Mann
John Marshall
Samuel Finley Breese Morse
George Peabody
Joseph Story
Gilbert Charles Stuart

George Washington
Daniel Webster
Eli Whitney

1905

John Quincy Adams
James Russell Lowell
Mary Lyon
James Madison
Maria Mitchell
William Tecumseh Sherman
John Greenleaf Whittier
Emma Willard

1910

George Bancroft
Phillips Brooks
William Cullen Bryant
James Fenimore Cooper
Oliver Wendell Holmes
Andrew Jackson
John Lothrop Motley
Edgar Allan Poe
Harriet Beecher Stowe
Frances Elizabeth Willard

1915

Louis Agassiz
Daniel Boone
Rufus Choate
Charlotte Saunders Cushman
Alexander Hamilton
Joseph Henry
Mark Hopkins
Elias Howe
Francis Parkman

1920

Samuel Langhorne Clemens
(Mark Twain)
James Buchanan Eads
Patrick Henry
William Thomas Green Morton
Alice Freeman Palmer
Augustus Saint-Gaudens
Roger Williams

1925

Edwin Booth
John Paul Jones

1930

Matthew Fontaine Maury
James Monroe
James Abbott McNeill Whistler
Walt Whitman

1935

Grover Cleveland
Simon Newcomb
William Penn

1940

Stephen Collins Foster

1945

Sidney Lanier
Thomas Paine
Walter Reed
Booker T. Washington

1950

Susan B. Anthony
Alexander Graham Bell
Josiah Willard Gibbs
William Crawford Gorgas
Theodore Roosevelt
Woodrow Wilson

1955

Thomas Jonathan "Stonewall"
Jackson
George Westinghouse
Wilbur Wright

1960

Thomas Alva Edison
Edward Alexander MacDowell
Henry David Thoreau

With the exception of Wilbur Wright, Edward Alexander Mac-Dowell, and Henry David Thoreau, all the above have the permanent tribute of the bronze tablet and portrait bust.

Chronology of Ceremonies

From time to time the Director invites appropriate organizations or individuals to present the bronze busts of persons who have been elected to the Hall of Fame. Eighty-six of the persons thus far honored have the permanent tributes of the bronzes. The dates of unveiling ceremonies are below:

MAY 30, 1907

Horace Mann (Bust replaced by original work in May, 1930)

SEPTEMBER 29, 1909

Robert Fulton

APRIL 27, 1922

Ulysses Simpson Grant (Replaced by another bust in May, 1923)

MAY 20, 1922

Mark Hopkins
Maria Mitchell
Edgar Allan Poe
Gilbert Charles Stuart
George Washington

MAY 22, 1923

Henry Ward Beecher
Ralph Waldo Emerson
Ulysses Simpson Grant
Alexander Hamilton
Robert Edward Lee

Abraham Lincoln
Frances Elizabeth Willard

MAY 13, 1924

John Adams
Phillips Brooks
Samuel Langhorne Clemens
  (Mark Twain)
Peter Cooper
James Buchanan Eads
Joseph Henry
Andrew Jackson
Thomas Jefferson
William Thomas Green Morton
Alice Freeman Palmer

MAY 21, 1925

Charlotte Saunders Cushman
Asa Gray
John Marshall
William Tecumseh Sherman
Harriet Beecher Stowe

MAY 12, 1926

Daniel Boone
Edwin Booth
Jonathan Edwards
James Kent

George Peabody
Augustus Saint-Gaudens
Daniel Webster
Eli Whitney
Roger Williams

MAY 5, 1927

John James Audubon
William Ellery Channing
David Glasgow Farragut
Benjamin Franklin
Washington Irving
Mary Lyon

MAY 10, 1928

Louis Agassiz
Rufus Choate
John Paul Jones
Samuel Finley Breese Morse
John Greenleaf Whittier

MAY 9, 1929

William Cullen Bryant
Henry Clay
Nathaniel Hawthorne
Oliver Wendell Holmes
Henry Wadsworth Longfellow
James Madison
Francis Parkman
Emma Willard

MAY 8, 1930

John Quincy Adams
George Bancroft
James Fenimore Cooper
Patrick Henry
Elias Howe
James Russell Lowell
Horace Mann
John Lothrop Motley
Joseph Story

MAY 14, 1931

Matthew Fontaine Maury
James Monroe
James Abbott McNeill Whistler
Walt Whitman

FEBRUARY 22, 1932

Bicentenary of the birth of Washington and presentation of a replica of Houdon's bust of Lafayette placed opposite the Hall of Fame; presentation of the bust by Dr. Robert Underwood Johnson, Director of the Hall of Fame; acknowledgment by Comte René de Chambrun, representing the family of LaFayette; tributes to LaFayette by Dr. Sébastien Charléty, Rector of the University of Paris (de l'Institut de France); M. André Chevrillon (de l'Académie Française); and Colonel François Pillon, Military Attaché of the French Embassy, representing His Excellency M. Paul Claudel, French Ambassador; tributes to Washington by Hon. Samuel Seabury and Miss Agnes Repplier; Dr. Edwin Markham's poem "Washington the Nation Builder" was read by the poet; music by Edward Johnson and the Gloria Trumpeters.

MAY 28, 1936

Simon Newcomb
William Penn

MARCH 18, 1937

Grover Cleveland

MAY 27, 1941

Stephen Collins Foster

MAY 23, 1946

Booker T. Washington

OCTOBER 3, 1946

Sidney Lanier

MAY 20, 1948

Walter Reed

MAY 24, 1951

Alexander Graham Bell
William Crawford Gorgas

MAY 18, 1952

Susan B. Anthony
Thomas Paine

MAY 9, 1954

Theodore Roosevelt

MAY 20, 1956

Woodrow Wilson

MAY 19, 1957

Thomas Jonathan "Stonewall"
    Jackson

DECEMBER 1, 1957

Josiah Willard Gibbs
George Westinghouse

JUNE 4, 1961

Thomas Alva Edison

The North Gate to the Colonnade.

Record

OF THE RESULTS OF THE
THIRTEEN QUINQUENNIAL ELECTIONS
1900 - 1960

Until 1920 and inclusive of that election, candidates were ineligible until ten years after death; in 1922, the ten-year requirement was increased to twenty-five years.

In the elections from 1900-1920, a majority vote of the Electors (approximately 100) was necessary to a choice of a candidate. In 1922, the ruling was changed to require a three-fifths vote of the Electors. However, prior to the 1945 election, it was deemed advisable to revert to the majority ruling, which is in effect today.

A dash (—) under an election year indicates that the candidate was not nominated and therefore not considered by the College of Electors that year.

I — Authors

NAMES CHOSEN

	1900	1905	1910	1915	1920	1925	1930	1935	1940	1945	1950	1955	1960
George Bancroft	—	40	53	—	—	—	—	—	—	—	—	—	—
William Cullen Bryant	49	43	59	—	—	—	—	—	—	—	—	—	—
Samuel Langhorne Clemens (Mark Twain)	—	—	—	—	72	—	—	—	—	—	—	—	—
James Fenimore Cooper	30	43	62	—	—	—	—	—	—	—	—	—	—
Ralph Waldo Emerson	87	—	—	—	—	—	—	—	—	—	—	—	—
Nathaniel Hawthorne	73	—	—	—	—	—	—	—	—	—	—	—	—
Oliver Wendell Holmes	—	49	69	—	—	—	—	—	—	—	—	—	—
Washington Irving	83	—	—	—	—	—	—	—	—	—	—	—	—
Sidney Lanier	—	—	—	—	—	26	20	55	60	48	—	—	—
Henry Wadsworth Longfellow	85	—	—	—	—	—	—	—	—	—	—	—	—
James Russell Lowell	—	59	—	—	—	—	—	—	—	—	—	—	—
John Lothrop Motley	41	47	51	—	—	—	—	—	—	—	—	—	—
Thomas Paine	—	—	—	—	32	—	36	15	50	51	—	—	—
Francis Parkman	—	47	45	68	—	—	—	—	—	—	—	—	—
Edgar Allan Poe	38	42	69	—	—	—	—	—	—	—	—	—	—
Harriet Beecher Stowe	—	—	74	—	—	—	—	—	—	—	—	—	—
Henry David Thoreau	—	—	—	—	—	—	—	—	—	—	—	—	83
Walt Whitman	—	—	—	10	20	44	64	—	—	—	—	—	—
John Greenleaf Whittier	—	53	—	—	—	—	—	—	—	—	—	—	—

NAMES NOT CHOSEN

	1900	1905	1910	1915	1920	1925	1930	1935	1940	1945	1950	1955	1960
Abigail Smith Adams	—	25	18	13	9	—	—	—	—	—	—	0	—
Henry Adams	—	—	—	—	—	—	—	—	—	—	—	1	3
Louisa May Alcott	—	37	38	44	57	—	—	28	23	1	2	0	0
Elizabeth Cary Agassiz	—	—	—	—	3	—	—	—	—	—	—	—	—
Thomas Bailey Aldrich°	—	—	—	—	5	—	—	—	—	2	—	—	—
Horatio Alger	—	—	—	—	—	—	—	—	—	—	—	0	0
Katherine Lee Bates	—	—	—	—	—	—	—	—	—	—	—	0	—
Frederick Converse Beach	—	—	—	—	—	—	—	—	—	0	—	—	—
Edward Bellamy	—	—	—	—	—	—	—	—	—	—	0	—	—
Ambrose Bierce	—	—	—	—	—	—	—	—	—	—	—	—	0
Alice Cary	—	14	13	6	10	—	—	—	—	—	—	—	—
Phoebe Cary	—	12	11	3	7	—	—	—	—	—	—	—	—
George Catlin	—	—	—	—	—	—	0	—	—	—	—	—	—
Stephen Crane	—	—	—	—	—	1	1	—	—	—	—	0	0
Francis Marion Crawford°	—	—	—	—	2	—	—	—	—	—	—	—	—
George William Curtis	—	8	26	6	4	—	—	—	—	—	—	—	0
Charles A. Dana	—	—	—	—	1	—	—	—	—	0	—	—	—
Emily Dickinson	—	—	—	—	—	—	—	—	19	6	7	14	11
Mary Mapes Dodge	—	—	—	—	—	—	—	—	—	0	—	—	—
Paul Laurence Dunbar	—	—	—	—	—	—	—	—	—	—	0	0	1
Daniel Decatur Emmet	—	—	—	—	—	—	0	—	—	—	—	—	—
Eugene Field	—	—	—	—	4	—	—	—	—	—	0	—	—

I—AUTHORS [Continued]

	1900	1905	1910	1915	1920	1925	1930	1935	1940	1945	1950	1955	1960
John Fiske	—	—	—	8	11	—	—	—	3	0	—	—	—
John Fox, Jr.	—	—	—	—	—	—	—	—	—	—	—	0	—
Philip Freneau	—	—	—	—	—	—	—	—	0	0	—	0	—
Sarah Margaret Fuller	—	23	31	28	28	—	—	—	—	—	0	—	—
Henry George	—	—	—	—	3	—	30	56	47	25	11	6	1
Richard Watson Gilder*	—	—	—	—	5	—	—	4	—	—	—	—	—
Henry Woodfin Grady	—	—	—	—	—	—	—	—	8	—	—	—	0
Horace Greeley	45	35	30	14	7	—	—	—	8	0	0	7	8
Sarah Josepha Buell Hale	—	—	—	—	—	—	—	1					
Joel Chandler Harris	—	—	—	—	10	—	—	31	19	—	1	1	0
Francis Bret Harte	—	—	—	6	5	—	—	—	11	—	0	2	0
Richard Hildreth	1	—	—	—	—	—	1	—	—	—	—	—	—
Josiah Gilbert Holland	—	—	—	—	—	—	—	—	—	0	—	—	—
Julia Ward Howe	—	—	—	—	—	—	—	—	8	2	0	—	—
William Dean Howells	—	—	—	—	—	—	—	—	—	—	2	3	0
Elbert Hubbard	—	—	—	—	—	—	—	—	0	—	—	0	0
Henry Inman	—	—	—	—	—	—	—	—	—	—	—	0	—
Helen Hunt Jackson	3	34	31	25	37	—	—	—	—	—	—	—	—
Henry James, Jr.	—	—	—	—	—	—	—	—	—	2	10	—	4
William James	—	—	—	—	—	—	—	—	35	12	33	57	43
Francis Scott Key	2	6	5	5	3	—	6	—	11	0	0	2	1
Joyce Kilmer	—	—	—	—	—	—	—	—	—	0	0	0	0
Eugene Lawrence	—	—	—	—	—	—	—	—	—	—	—	—	0
Emma Lazarus	—	—	—	—	—	—	—	—	0	—	0	—	0
Francis Lieber	—	—	—	—	6	—	—	—	—	—	—	—	—
Nicholas Vachel Lindsay	—	—	—	—	—	—	—	—	—	—	—	—	0
Jack London	—	—	—	—	—	—	—	—	—	0	0	—	0
Amy Lowell	—	—	—	—	—	—	—	—	—	—	—	0	—
John Charles McNeill	—	—	—	—	—	—	—	—	—	—	—	—	0
Herman Melville	—	—	—	—	—	—	—	24	23	5	9	16	22
Joaquin Miller	—	—	—	—	—	—	—	—	—	0	0	—	—
S. Weir Mitchell	—	—	—	—	—	—	—	—	5	1	0	—	0
Mary Noailles Murfree	—	—	—	—	—	—	—	—	—	—	—	—	0
Charles Eliot Norton	—	—	—	—	2	—	—	—	—	—	—	—	—
John Boyle O'Reilly	—	—	—	—	—	—	—	—	0	—	0	—	—
William Sidney Porter (O. Henry)	—	—	—	—	—	—	—	—	7	—	1	1	0
William Hickling Prescott	33	27	21	16	18	—	—	—	8	1	—	0	2
Margaret Preston	—	—	—	—	—	—	0	—	—	—	—	—	—
Joseph Pulitzer	—	—	—	—	—	—	—	—	2	—	0	2	0
Eugene Marlove Rhodes	—	—	—	—	—	—	—	—	—	—	—	—	0
John Clark Ridpath	—	—	—	—	—	—	—	—	—	0	—	—	—
James Whitcomb Riley	—	—	—	—	—	—	—	—	—	3	3	4	1
Henry Martyn Robert	—	—	—	—	—	—	—	—	—	—	0	—	—
Lydia Hunt Sigourney	1	12	8	0	1	—	—	—	—	—	—	—	—
Evangelinus Apostolides Sophocles	—	—	—	—	—	—	0	—	—	—	—	—	—
William Graham Sumner	—	—	—	—	—	—	—	—	9	—	—	—	—

* Ineligible when voted for.

I—AUTHORS [*Continued*]

	1900	1905	1910	1915	1920	1925	1930	1935	1940	1945	1950	1955	1960
Bayard Taylor	—	—	—	—	—	—	—	—	—	—	—	—	0
Thorstein B. Veblen	—	—	—	—	—	—	—	—	—	—	—	0	—
Lew Wallace	—	—	—	—	—	—	—	—	0	—	—	0	0
Henry Watterson	—	—	—	—	—	—	—	—	—	—	—	—	0
Noah Webster	36	34	38	30	29	50	27	28	34	4	4	2	1
Phillis Wheatley	—	—	—	—	—	—	—	—	—	—	—	0	—
William Dwight Whitney	—	7	9	3	2	—	—	—	—	—	—	—	—
Ella Wheeler Wilcox	—	—	—	—	—	—	—	—	—	0	0	—	—
Alexander Wilson	—	—	—	—	—	—	—	0	—	—	—	—	0
Constance Fenimore Woolson	3	7	6	1	4	—	—	—	—	—	—	—	—
Chauncey Wright	—	—	—	—	—	—	—	—	0	—	—	—	—

II — Educators

NAMES CHOSEN

	1900	1905	1910	1915	1920	1925	1930	1935	1940	1945	1950	1955	1960
Mark Hopkins	48	40	45	69	—	—	—	—	—	—	—	—	—
Mary Lyon	20	59	—	—	—	—	—	—	—	—	—	—	—
Horace Mann	67	—	—	—	—	—	—	—	—	—	—	—	—
Alice Freeman Palmer	—	—	—	47	53	—	—	—	—	—	—	—	—
Booker T. Washington	—	—	—	—	—	—	—	—	57	57	—	—	—
Emma Willard°	4	50	—	—	—	—	—	—	—	—	—	—	—

NAMES NOT CHOSEN

	1900	1905	1910	1915	1920	1925	1930	1935	1940	1945	1950	1955	1960
Samuel Chapman Armstrong	—	—	—	—	10	—	8	—	—	—	—	—	0
Henry Barnard	—	—	—	—	—	—	23	33	16	—	0	—	—
William H. H. Beadle	—	—	—	—	—	—	—	—	—	—	—	—	0
Bordon Parker Bowne	—	—	—	—	11	—	—	1	—	—	—	—	—
Alexander Campbell	—	—	—	—	—	—	—	—	—	—	—	—	0
George Fisk Comfort	—	—	—	—	—	—	—	—	1	—	—	—	—
Russell Hermann Conwell	—	—	—	—	—	—	—	—	—	—	—	—	0
Prudence Crandall	—	—	—	—	—	—	—	—	—	—	—	—	0
Charles W. Eliot	—	—	—	—	—	—	—	—	—	—	—	20	23
Edward Miner Gallaudet	—	—	—	—	—	—	—	—	—	—	—	—	0
Thomas Hopkins Gallaudet	14	8	5	5	7	—	5	—	—	—	—	—	—
Daniel Coit Gilman	—	—	—	—	11	—	—	—	—	—	—	4	—
Mentor Graham	—	—	—	—	—	—	—	—	—	0	—	—	—
George Guess (Sequoyah)	—	—	—	—	—	—	—	—	—	—	—	0	0
William Rainey Harper	—	—	—	—	—	—	—	—	—	—	3	5	4
William Torrey Harris	—	—	—	—	—	—	—	—	5	—	—	—	—
Ezra L'Hommedieu	—	—	—	—	—	—	—	—	0	—	0	—	—
Samuel G. Howe	9	6	10	9	7	—	—	—	—	—	—	—	—
Richard Henry Jesse	—	—	—	—	—	—	—	—	—	—	—	—	0
Joseph LeConte	—	—	—	—	—	—	—	10	—	—	—	—	—
Seth Low	—	—	—	—	—	—	—	—	—	—	—	—	0
Henry Mitchell MacCracken	—	—	—	—	—	—	—	—	—	0	0	—	—
William H. McGuffey	5	—	—	—	2	—	—	17	—	—	2	—	—

II—EDUCATORS [*Continued*]

	1900	1905	1910	1915	1920	1925	1930	1935	1940	1945	1950	1955	1960
Eliphalet Nott	—	—	—	—	3	—	2	—	—	—	0	—	—
James Kennedy Patterson	—	—	—	—	—	—	—	—	—	—	—	1	—
Elizabeth A. Seton	0	—	—	—	2	—	—	—	0	—	0	1	0
Edward Austin Sheldon	—	—	—	—	—	—	—	1	0	—	—	—	—
Charles Sprague Smith	—	—	—	—	—	—	—	—	0	—	—	—	—
Henry Philip Tappan	7	—	—	—	—	—	1	—	—	—	—	—	—
William Tennent	—	—	—	—	—	—	—	—	—	—	—	—	0
Sylvanus Thayer	—	—	—	—	—	—	—	3	9	2	—	—	70
Eben Tourjee	—	—	—	—	—	—	—	—	—	—	—	—	0
Moses Coit Tyler	—	—	—	—	—	—	—	—	1	—	—	—	—
Francis Wayland	24	17	19	13	13	—	—	—	—	—	—	—	—
John Witherspoon	—	3	6	4	4	—	10	—	—	—	—	—	0
Theodore Dwight Woolsey	21	11	10	3	7	—	—	—	—	—	—	—	—

*In the year 1905 there were 95 Electors, thus requiring but 48 votes for election.

III — Preachers, Theologians

NAMES CHOSEN

	1900	1905	1910	1915	1920	1925	1930	1935	1940	1945	1950	1955	1960
Henry Ward Beecher	64	—	—	—	—	—	—	—	—	—	—	—	—
Phillips Brooks	—	49	60	—	—	—	—	—	—	—	—	—	—
William Ellery Channing	58	—	—	—	—	—	—	—	—	—	—	—	—
Jonathan Edwards	82	—	—	—	—	—	—	—	—	—	—	—	—
Roger Williams	—	—	—	26	66	—	—	—	—	—	—	—	—

NAMES NOT CHOSEN

	1900	1905	1910	1915	1920	1925	1930	1935	1940	1945	1950	1955	1960
Richard Allen	—	—	—	—	—	—	—	—	—	—	—	—	0
Francis Asbury	—	8	7	2	3	—	15	—	12	2	1	—	0
Hosea Ballou	—	—	—	—	—	—	—	—	—	—	—	—	0
Lyman Beecher	4	8	7	4	1	—	—	—	—	—	—	—	—
William Brewster	—	5	5	1	1	—	—	1	—	1	—	—	1
Peter Bulkeley	—	—	—	—	—	—	—	1	—	—	0	—	—
Horace Bushnell	32	23	19	42	33	27	18	—	—	0	—	0	—
John Carroll	—	—	—	—	—	—	—	—	—	—	0	0	0
Peter Cartwright	—	—	—	—	—	—	—	—	—	0	0	—	—
William Cummins Davis	—	—	—	—	—	—	—	—	—	—	—	—	0
Palmer Dyer	—	—	—	—	—	—	—	—	0	—	—	—	—
John England	—	—	—	—	—	—	—	—	—	—	—	—	0
Robert Feeks	—	—	—	—	—	—	—	—	0	0	—	—	—
James Cardinal Gibbons	—	—	—	—	—	—	—	—	—	—	0	1	3
Edward Everett Hale	—	—	—	—	13	—	—	—	—	1	—	—	—
John Harvard	—	—	—	—	—	—	—	—	—	0	—	3	—
Thomas Hooker	—	—	—	—	—	—	—	—	—	—	—	—	0
John Ireland	—	—	—	—	—	—	—	—	—	—	0	—	1

III—PREACHERS, THEOLOGIANS [*Continued*]

	1900	1905	1910	1915	1920	1925	1930	1935	1940	1945	1950	1955	1960
Louis Klopsch	—	—	—	—	—	—	—	—	—	—	—	—	0
Elijah Parish Lovejoy	—	—	—	—	—	—	—	—	—	—	0	1	0
Cotton Mather	18	8	11	2	1	—	—	—	—	0	—	—	—
John N. Neumann	—	—	—	—	—	—	—	—	—	—	—	—	1
Samuel Charles Mazzuchelli	—	—	—	—	—	—	—	—	—	—	0	0	—
Dwight Lyman Moody	—	—	—	8	8	—	—	—	—	—	2	4	0
Heinrich Melchior Muhlenberg	—	—	—	—	1	—	—	—	—	—	—	—	—
William Augustus Muhlenberg	—	—	—	—	—	—	0	—	—	—	—	—	—
Theodore Parker	21	11	10	9	7	—	6	—	—	—	1	—	—
Gabriel Richard	—	—	—	—	—	—	—	—	—	—	0	0	0
Matthew Simpson	11	29	20	10	7	—	—	—	—	—	—	0	—
Joseph Smith	—	—	—	—	—	—	0	—	1	—	—	—	1
Judah Touro	—	—	—	—	—	—	—	—	—	—	—	—	1
Isaac N. Wise	—	—	—	—	—	—	10	—	—	—	—	—	—
John Woolman	—	—	—	—	—	—	6	—	8	—	—	—	—
Brigham Young	—	—	—	—	—	—	—	—	—	—	—	—	1

IV—Humanitarians, Social and Economic Reformers

NAMES CHOSEN

	1900	1905	1910	1915	1920	1925	1930	1935	1940	1945	1950	1955	1960
Susan B. Anthony	—	—	—	—	46	—	—	55	40	40	72	—	—
Frances Elizabeth Willard	—	—	55	—	—	—	—	—	—	—	—	—	—

NAMES NOT CHOSEN

	1900	1905	1910	1915	1920	1925	1930	1935	1940	1945	1950	1955	1960
Jane Addams	—	—	—	—	—	—	—	—	—	—	—	—	69
Michael Anagnos	—	—	—	—	—	—	—	—	—	—	—	—	0
Lord Baltimore, 2nd (Cecil Calvert)	—	—	—	—	—	—	—	—	2	—	—	—	—
Henry Bergh	—	—	—	—	7	—	—	—	—	—	—	—	—
Alice McLellan Birney	—	—	—	—	—	—	0	—	—	—	—	—	—
Lucy Stone Blackwell	—	10	7	9	12	—	—	0	—	—	0	2	—
Helena Petrovna Blavatsky	—	—	—	—	—	—	—	0	2	—	—	—	—
Edward W. Bok	—	—	—	—	—	—	—	—	—	—	—	0	0
John Brown°	17	7	16	9	21	—	—	—	—	0	0	—	0
Elihu Burritt	—	—	—	—	—	—	—	—	—	—	—	—	0
Frances Xavier Cabrini	—	—	—	—	—	—	—	—	—	—	0	0	1
Lydia Maria Child	—	—	—	—	—	—	2	—	—	—	—	—	—
Cornelia Connelly	—	—	—	—	—	—	—	—	—	—	—	0	—
Ann Pamela Cunningham	—	—	—	14	15	—	—	—	—	—	—	—	—
Eleanor Dare	—	8	6	1	1	—	—	—	—	—	—	—	—
Eugene Debs	—	—	—	—	—	—	—	—	—	—	—	0	0
Dorothea Lynde Dix	12	37	29	28	31	27	7	—	19	2	13	10	4
Frederick Douglass	—	—	—	—	—	—	4	3	8	0	1	4	6

IV—HUMANITARIANS, SOCIAL AND ECONOMIC REFORMERS [*Continued*]

	1900	1905	1910	1915	1920	1925	1930	1935	1940	1945	1950	1955	1960
Joseph Dutton	—	—	—	—	—	—	—	—	—	—	—	—	0
Mary Dyer	—	6	6	2	3	—	1	—	—	—	—	—	—
Mary Baker Eddy	—	—	—	—	—	—	—	—	5	0	2	0	1
William Lloyd Garrison	19	20	35	14	11	32	12	—	—	—	5	3	2
Samuel Gompers	—	—	—	—	—	—	—	—	—	—	1	7	5
Isabella Hardenburg (Sojourner Truth)	—	—	—	—	—	—	—	—	—	—	0	—	—
Anne Hutchinson	—	20	6	6	9	—	—	—	—	—	—	—	—
Elizabeth E. Hutter	—	—	—	—	—	—	—	0	—	—	—	—	—
Chief Joseph (of Nez Perce)	—	—	—	—	—	—	—	—	—	—	—	—	0
William Ladd	—	—	—	—	—	—	—	—	—	—	—	—	0
Rose Hawthorne Lathrop	—	—	—	—	—	—	—	—	—	—	—	0	0
Sophie Irene Loeb	—	—	—	—	—	—	—	—	—	—	—	0	0
Juliette G. Low	—	—	—	—	—	—	—	—	—	—	—	0	0
Josephine Shaw Lowell	—	—	—	—	—	—	—	—	—	—	—	—	0
Dorothy Payne Madison	—	16	23	13	8	—	—	—	—	—	—	—	—
Mary P. Mann	—	—	—	—	—	—	—	—	—	—	—	0	—
John Mitchell	—	—	—	—	—	—	—	—	—	—	—	—	0
Esther Hobart Morris	—	—	—	—	—	—	—	—	—	—	0	—	—
Thomas Morris	—	—	—	—	—	0	—	—	—	—	—	—	—
Lucretia Coffin Mott	11	33	41	40	46	—	—	5	3	4	1	2	2
Carry Nation	—	—	—	—	—	—	—	—	0	—	—	—	—
Wendell Phillips	19	17	20	5	8	19	11	—	10	—	1	—	0
Leonidas Lafayette Polk	—	—	—	—	—	—	—	—	—	—	—	—	1
Jacob Riis	—	—	—	—	—	—	—	—	—	—	0	—	—
Ernestine L. Rose	—	—	—	—	—	—	—	—	—	—	—	—	0
Abram Joseph Ryan	—	—	—	—	—	—	—	—	—	—	—	—	0
Anna Howard Shaw	—	—	—	—	—	—	—	—	—	—	—	—	0
Sophia Smith	—	—	—	—	—	—	—	—	—	—	—	—	0
Elizabeth Cady Stanton	—	—	—	—	20	—	—	3	3	0	1	3	1
Lucy Stone	—	—	—	—	—	—	—	—	—	—	—	—	0
Jonathan Walker	—	—	—	—	—	—	—	—	—	—	—	—	0
Martha Washington	14	32	43	35	38	—	7	—	—	—	—	0	—
Mary Washington	—	19	23	9	4	—	—	—	—	—	—	—	—
Anna Zenger	—	—	—	—	—	—	—	—	—	—	—	0	—
John Peter Zenger	—	—	—	—	—	—	—	—	—	—	1	5	0

*Until 1920 Brown was balloted for in Class XVI. In 1925 his name was not on the ballot reported by the Committee on Nominations.

V—Scientists

NAMES CHOSEN

	1900	1905	1910	1915	1920	1925	1930	1935	1940	1945	1950	1955	1960
Louis Agassiz	—	—	—	65	—	—	—	—	—	—	—	—	—
John James Audubon	67	—	—	—	—	—	—	—	—	—	—	—	—
Josiah Willard Gibbs	—	—	—	—	9	—	40	55	56	36	64	—	—
Asa Gray	51	—	—	—	—	—	—	—	—	—	—	—	—
Joseph Henry	44	34	39	56	—	—	—	—	—	—	—	—	—

V—SCIENTISTS [Continued]

	1900	1905	1910	1915	1920	1925	1930	1935	1940	1945	1950	1955	1960
Matthew Fontaine Maury	20	14	11	13	20	52	66	—	—	—	—	—	—
Maria Mitchell°	7	48	—	—	—	—	—	—	—	—	—	—	—
Simon Newcomb	—	—	—	—	44	—	—	78	—	—	—	—	—

NAMES NOT CHOSEN

	1900	1905	1910	1915	1920	1925	1930	1935	1940	1945	1950	1955	1960
Spencer Fullerton Baird	8	5	7	2	1	—	3	—	—	—	—	—	—
John Bartram	—	—	—	—	—	—	—	—	—	—	0	2	0
Nathaniel Bowditch	10	8	11	4	3	—	—	7	—	—	—	0	—
James Dwight Dana	—	—	—	—	—	—	—	—	—	—	0	—	—
Grove Karl Gilbert	—	—	—	—	—	—	—	—	—	—	0	—	—
Ebon Norton Horsford	—	—	—	—	—	—	0	—	—	—	—	—	—
Seaman A. Knapp	—	—	—	—	—	—	—	—	—	—	—	7	3
Samuel Pierpont Langley	—	—	—	—	20	—	—	—	—	2	1	—	—
Joseph Leidy	—	—	—	—	—	—	9	—	—	—	—	—	—
Albert Abraham Michelson	—	—	—	—	—	—	—	—	—	—	—	—	2
Benjamin Peirce	14	12	8	1	3	—	—	—	—	—	1	1	—
Charles Saunders Peirce	—	—	—	—	—	—	—	—	—	—	2	3	—
Edward Charles Pickering	—	—	—	—	—	—	—	—	—	—	0	—	—
James Wesley Powell	—	—	—	—	—	—	—	—	—	—	0	—	—
Joseph Priestley	—	—	—	—	—	—	—	—	—	—	2	—	—
Theodore William Richards	—	—	—	—	—	—	—	—	—	—	—	0	—
Henry Augustus Rowland	—	—	—	—	—	—	—	—	—	—	0	—	—
Benjamin Silliman	17	7	8	1	2	—	—	—	—	—	—	—	—
Lyman Spalding	—	—	—	—	—	—	3	0	—	—	—	—	—
Benjamin Thompson	19	20	26	31	38	24	8	—	—	—	—	—	—
Addison Emery Verrill	—	—	—	—	—	—	—	—	—	—	—	—	0
Israel Charles White	—	—	—	—	—	—	—	—	—	—	—	0	—
Charles Otis Whitman	—	—	—	—	—	—	—	—	—	—	0	—	—

* In the year 1905 there were 95 Electors, thus requiring but 48 votes for a majority.

VI—Engineers, Architects

NAMES CHOSEN

	1900	1905	1910	1915	1920	1925	1930	1935	1940	1945	1950	1955	1960
James Buchanan Eads	41	18	16	28	51	—	—	—	—	—	—	—	—

NAMES NOT CHOSEN

	1900	1905	1910	1915	1920	1925	1930	1935	1940	1945	1950	1955	1960
Henry Bacon	—	—	—	—	—	—	—	—	—	—	0	—	—
Benjamin Banneker	—	—	—	—	—	—	—	—	—	—	0	1	0
Louise Bethune	—	—	—	—	—	—	—	—	—	—	0	—	—
Charles Bulfinch	7	—	—	—	—	15	26	13	25	3	—	—	—
Octave Chanute	—	—	—	—	—	—	—	—	—	—	0	—	—
Edwin Laurentine Drake	—	—	—	—	—	—	—	—	—	—	0	—	0

VI—ENGINEERS, ARCHITECTS [Continued]

	1900	1905	1910	1915	1920	1925	1930	1935	1940	1945	1950	1955	1960
Cass Gilbert	—	—	—	—	—	—	—	—	—	—	—	—	0
Charles Thompson Harvey	—	—	—	—	—	—	—	—	—	—	0	—	—
Alexander Lyman Holley	8	1	15	4	0	—	2	—	—	—	—	—	—
Robert Woolston Hunt	—	—	—	—	—	—	—	—	—	—	—	—	0
John Bloomfield Jervis	1	—	—	—	—	—	—	0	—	—	—	—	—
Francis Hatch Kimball	—	—	—	—	—	—	—	—	—	0	0	—	0
Charles Follen McKim	—	—	—	—	7	—	—	44	18	—	—	—	—
Henry Hobson Richardson	32	20	15	11	11	26	4	7	6	—	—	—	—
John Augustus Roebling	—	10	6	4	2	—	—	—	—	—	—	—	—
Elmer Sperry	—	—	—	—	—	—	—	—	—	—	—	—	0
Charles P. Steinmetz	—	—	—	—	—	—	—	—	—	—	3	6	4
John Stevens	2	—	—	—	3	—	—	—	—	—	—	—	—

VII—Physicians, Surgeons

NAMES CHOSEN

	1900	1905	1910	1915	1920	1925	1930	1935	1940	1945	1950	1955	1960
William Crawford Gorgas	—	—	—	—	—	—	—	—	—	3	81	—	—
William Thomas Green Morton	6	29	36	37	72	—	—	—	—	—	—	—	—
Walter Reed	—	—	—	—	14	33	42	57	63	49	—	—	—

NAMES NOT CHOSEN

	1900	1905	1910	1915	1920	1925	1930	1935	1940	1945	1950	1955	1960
William Beaumont	—	—	—	—	—	—	16	—	7	2	1	2	1
William T. H. Bellamy	—	—	—	—	—	—	—	—	—	0	—	—	—
Elizabeth Blackwell	—	—	—	—	—	—	—	—	—	0	1	0	14
William Tillinghast Bull	—	—	—	—	1	—	—	—	—	—	—	—	—
John Murray Carnochan	—	—	—	—	1	—	—	—	—	—	—	—	—
Reginald Heber Fitz	—	—	—	—	—	—	—	—	0	—	—	—	—
Joseph Goldberger	—	—	—	—	—	—	—	—	—	—	—	—	0
William Stewart Halsted	—	—	—	—	—	—	—	—	—	—	0	—	1
Charles T. Jackson	—	—	—	—	10	—	—	—	—	—	—	—	—
Aloysius O. J. Kelly	—	—	—	—	—	—	—	—	—	—	—	0	—
Jesse W. Lazear	—	—	—	—	—	—	—	—	2	—	—	—	—
Crawford W. Long	—	—	—	11	4	—	—	—	—	—	1	2	2
William W. Mayo	—	—	—	—	—	—	—	—	—	—	—	4	4
Ephraim McDowell	5	1	5	2	1	—	3	—	2	0	0	2	—
John McLoughlin	—	—	—	—	—	—	—	—	—	—	—	—	0
John Benjamin Murphy	—	—	—	—	—	—	—	—	—	—	0	—	—
Howard Taylor Ricketts	—	—	—	—	—	—	—	—	—	—	1	—	—
Benjamin Rush	42	24	21	13	14	51	24	11	—	5	—	9	3
James Marion Sims	28	20	14	8	7	—	11	—	—	—	—	—	—
Nathan Smith	—	—	—	—	—	—	—	—	—	—	0	—	—
Edward Livingston Trudeau	—	—	—	—	—	—	—	—	—	—	1	2	1
William Henry Welch	—	—	—	—	—	—	—	—	—	—	—	—	11
Harvey W. Wiley	—	—	—	—	—	—	—	—	—	—	—	7	9
Daniel Hale Williams	—	—	—	—	—	—	—	—	—	—	—	—	0

VIII — Inventors

NAMES CHOSEN

	1900	1905	1910	1915	1920	1925	1930	1935	1940	1945	1950	1955	1960
Alexander Graham Bell	—	—	—	—	—	—	—	—	—	—	70	—	—
Thomas Alva Edison	—	—	—	—	—	—	—	—	—	—	—	—	108
Robert Fulton	86	—	—	—	—	—	—	—	—	—	—	—	—
Elias Howe	47	29	28	61	—	—	—	—	—	—	—	—	—
Samuel F. B. Morse	82	—	—	—	—	—	—	—	—	—	—	—	—
George Westinghouse	—	—	—	—	—	—	—	—	38	44	34	62	—
Eli Whitney	69	—	—	—	—	—	—	—	—	—	—	—	—
Wilbur Wright	—	—	—	—	—	—	—	—	—	16	42	86	—

NAMES NOT CHOSEN

	1900	1905	1910	1915	1920	1925	1930	1935	1940	1945	1950	1955	1960
Edward Goodrich Acheson	—	—	—	—	—	—	—	—	—	—	—	—	0
Alfred Ely Beach	—	—	—	—	—	—	—	—	0	0	—	—	—
Ephraim Bee Beckett	—	—	—	—	—	—	—	—	—	—	0	—	—
Carl Borden	—	—	—	—	—	—	—	—	—	—	—	0	—
Mathew B. Brady	—	—	—	—	—	—	—	0	—	—	—	—	—
William Seward Burroughs	—	—	—	—	—	—	0	—	—	—	—	—	—
William Austin Burt	—	—	—	—	7	—	0	—	0	0	0	0	—
George Henry Corliss	—	7	6	3	3	—	—	—	—	—	—	—	—
John Philo Cowing	—	—	—	—	—	—	—	—	0	—	—	—	—
Charles Ferdinand Dowd	—	—	—	—	—	—	3	—	—	—	—	—	—
John Ericsson	—	—	—	12	10	—	34	12	—	1	—	—	—
John Fitch	—	—	—	—	—	—	7	13	4	—	—	0	—
Herman Frasch	—	—	—	—	—	—	—	—	—	—	—	0	0
Charles Edgar Fritts	—	—	—	—	—	—	—	0	—	—	—	—	—
Richard Jordan Gatling	—	—	—	—	—	—	—	0	—	—	—	—	—
Charles Goodyear	13	11	7	2	16	—	1	3	32	0	0	2	0
John Gorrie	—	—	—	—	—	—	—	—	—	0	0	0	—
Charles Martin Hall	—	—	—	—	—	—	—	—	—	0	0	—	—
Elwood Haynes	—	—	—	—	—	—	—	—	—	0	—	—	—
Richard Marsh Hoe	19	16	18	17	9	—	—	—	—	—	—	—	—
Edwin James Houston	—	—	—	—	—	—	—	—	0	0	—	—	—
Walter Hunt	—	—	—	—	—	—	—	0	—	—	—	—	—
Cyrus H. McCormick	25	20	16	28	43	—	53	55	45	5	6	10	1
Robert McCormick	—	—	7	3	0	—	—	2	—	0	—	1	—
Ottmar Mergenthaler	—	—	—	—	2	—	13	—	—	—	—	—	—
Elisha G. Otis	—	—	—	—	—	—	—	—	—	—	—	0	—
Charles Kasouth Pickles	—	—	—	—	—	—	—	—	—	—	—	—	0
Elias E. Ries	—	—	—	—	—	—	—	—	—	—	—	—	0
James Rumsey	—	—	—	—	—	—	—	1	—	—	—	—	—
Christopher L. Sholes	—	—	—	—	—	—	—	—	0	—	—	0	—
Henry Miller Shreve	—	—	—	—	—	—	—	—	—	—	0	—	—
Isaac Merritt Singer	—	—	—	—	—	—	2	—	—	—	—	—	—
Robert L. Stevens	—	—	—	—	1	—	—	—	—	—	—	—	—
Lewis Edson Waterman	—	—	—	—	—	—	—	0	1	—	—	—	—
Horace Wells	14	—	—	—	—	—	—	—	6	6	1	—	0
Orville Wright*	—	—	—	—	—	—	—	—	—	—	—	—	51

*Special ruling was made by the Senate of New York University to permit Wright to stand as a candidate before the required number of years after death.

IX — Missionaries, Explorers

NAMES CHOSEN

	1900	1905	1910	1915	1920	1925	1930	1935	1940	1945	1950	1955	1960
Daniel Boone	35	36	42	52	—	—	—	—	—	—	—	—	—

NAMES NOT CHOSEN

	1900	1905	1910	1915	1920	1925	1930	1935	1940	1945	1950	1955	1960
Christopher (Kit) Carson	—	—	—	—	—	—	5	—	3	—	0	0	0
William Clark	—	—	—	—	5	—	3	—	—	0	0	4	—
William F. Cody	—	—	—	—	—	—	—	—	—	0	0	0'	—
David Crockett	8	—	4	1	4	—	7	—	—	—	0	0	0
Pierre Jean De Smet	—	—	—	—	—	—	—	—	—	—	—	—	0
John Eliot	—	—	—	7	6	—	—	—	—	0	—	0	—
James Jerome Hill	—	—	—	—	—	—	—	—+	—	—	1	—	—
Adoniram Judson	36	13	15	29	29	27	13	—	—	—	—	—	—
Sarah Hall Boardman Judson	—	7	5	6	5	—	—	—	—	—	—	—	—
Elisha Kent Kane	22	5	7	3	4	—	5	4	3	—	—	12	—
Meriwether Lewis	14	14	13	7	7	—	—	—	13	0	5	11	2
Jacques Marquette	—	—	—	8	8	—	—	—	—	—	0	—	—
James Wilson Marshall	—	—	—	—	—	—	—	—	—	0	0	—	—
Robert E. Peary	—	—	—	—	—	—	—	—	—	—	2	9	1
Matthew C. Perry	—	—	—	—	—	—	4	—	—	—	—	—	—
Zebulon Montgomery Pike	—	—	—	—	—	—	—	—	—	—	0	—	—
Junipero Serra	—	—	—	—	—	—	—	—	5	—	—	—	1
Jedediah Smith	—	—	—	—	1	—	—	—	—	—	—	—	—
Henry H. Stanley	—	—	—	—	21	—	—	—	—	—	—	—	—
Joseph Ward	—	—	—	—	—	—	—	—	1	—	—	—	—
Marcus Whitman	19	8	5	3	4	—	—	—	—	—	0	0	0

X — The Military

NAMES CHOSEN

	1900	1905	1910	1915	1920	1925	1930	1935	1940	1945	1950	1955	1960
David Glasgow Farragut	79	—	—	—	—	—	—	—	—	—	—	—	—
Ulysses Simpson Grant	93	—	—	—	—	—	—	—	—	—	—	—	—
Thomas Jonathan "Stonewall" Jackson	23	24	18	24	38	53	34	27	34	11	24	72	—
John Paul Jones	—	—	—	26	44	68	—	—	—	—	—	—	—
Robert E. Lee	68	—	—	—	—	—	—	—	—	—	—	—	—
William Tecumseh Sherman	—	58	—	—	—	—	—	—	—	—	—	—	—

NAMES NOT CHOSEN

	1900	1905	1910	1915	1920	1925	1930	1935	1940	1945	1950	1955	1960
Ethan Allen	—	—	—	—	—	—	—	—	—	0	—	0	0
Crispus Attucks	—	—	—	—	—	—	—	—	—	—	—	0	—
Joshua Barney	—	—	—	—	—	—	1	—	—	—	—	—	—
John Barry	—	—	—	—	—	—	0	—	3	—	—	0	0

X—THE MILITARY [Continued]

	1900	1905	1910	1915	1920	1925	1930	1935	1940	1945	1950	1955	1960
James Bowie	—	—	—	—	—	—	—	—	—	0	—	—	—
George Rogers Clark	19	20	25	21	23	39	28	46	41	17	3	17	4
Benjamin Cleveland	—	—	—	—	—	—	—	—	—	—	0	—	—
Enoch Crosby	—	—	—	—	—	—	—	—	0	—	—	—	—
George A. Custer	—	—	—	—	—	—	—	—	3	0	—	0	—
Stephen Decatur	23	18	21	7	3	—	—	—	—	—	—	—	—
George Dewey	—	—	—	—	—	—	—	—	—	0	0	0	—
John Charles Fremont	17	7	13	2	1	—	10	—	—	—	0	0	0
Horatio Gates	—	—	—	—	—	—	—	—	—	0	—	—	0
Robert Gray	—	—	—	—	—	—	—	—	—	0	—	—	—
Nathanael Greene	30	34	25	37	38	38	21	11	12	—	—	0	—
Nathan Hale	5	12	20	7	2	—	14	—	—	—	3	3	1
Oliver Otis Howard	—	—	—	—	—	—	—	—	—	—	0	—	—
Andrew Atkinson Humphreys	—	—	—	—	—	—	0	—	—	—	—	—	—
Joshua Humphreys	—	—	—	—	—	—	0	—	—	—	—	—	—
Albert Sidney Johnston	12	9	5	0	2	—	—	—	—	—	—	—	—
Joseph E. Johnston	—	—	—	—	3	—	—	—	—	—	—	—	—
Stephen W. Kearny	—	—	—	—	—	—	—	—	—	—	—	0	—
Henry Knox	—	—	—	—	—	—	—	—	—	—	—	—	0
James Lawrence	—	—	—	—	—	—	—	—	—	—	—	0	—
Pierre Charles L'Enfant	—	—	—	—	—	—	—	—	—	—	—	—	0
James Longstreet	—	—	—	—	—	—	—	—	—	—	—	0	0
Frank Luke, Jr.	—	—	—	—	—	—	—	—	—	—	—	—	0
Thomas MacDonough	—	—	—	—	—	—	—	—	—	—	—	—	0
Francis Marion	—	—	—	—	—	—	—	—	—	—	—	—	1
George Gordon Meade	6	3	6	3	3	—	—	—	—	—	—	—	—
William Pepperrell	—	—	17	6	0	—	—	—	—	—	—	—	—
Oliver Hazard Perry	26	13	20	9	5	—	—	30	28	1	0	0	0
David Dixon Porter	6	2	7	0	0	—	—	—	—	—	—	—	—
Edward Preble	—	—	—	—	—	—	—	—	—	0	—	—	—
Sterling Price	—	—	—	—	—	—	0	—	—	—	—	—	—
Count Casimir Pulaski	—	—	—	—	—	—	—	—	—	—	—	—	1
Israel Putnam	10	—	—	—	—	—	2	—	—	—	—	—	—
Paul Revere	—	—	—	—	—	15	6	—	—	—	1	1	2
James Robertson	—	—	—	—	—	—	1	—	—	—	—	—	—
Winfield Scott Schley	—	—	—	—	—	—	—	—	0	—	—	—	—
Philip Schuyler	4	2	6	0	0	—	—	—	—	—	—	—	—
Winfield Scott	16	6	11	2	4	—	2	—	—	—	—	—	0
Philip Henry Sheridan	23	18	33	24	52	48	17	—	7	—	—	1	—
Frederick W. von Steuben	—	—	—	—	—	—	—	—	3	—	0	0	—
James Ewell Brown Stuart	—	—	—	—	—	—	—	—	—	—	—	—	0
Zachary Taylor	9	2	6	1	1	—	—	—	—	—	—	—	—
George Henry Thomas	24	19	18	10	9	—	6	5	—	0	0	—	0
Unknown Soldier	—	—	—	—	—	—	—	—	—	2	—	—	—
Anthony Wayne	—	—	—	—	—	—	—	—	3	—	—	—	—
Joseph Wheeler	—	—	—	—	—	—	—	—	—	—	—	0	—
Marcus J. Wright	—	—	—	—	—	—	—	—	—	—	—	—	0
Charles Young	—	—	—	—	—	—	—	—	—	—	—	0	—

XI — Lawyers, Judges

NAMES CHOSEN

	1900	1905	1910	1915	1920	1925	1930	1935	1940	1945	1950	1955	1960
Rufus Choate	47	31	28	52	—	—	—	—	—	—	—	—	—
James Kent	65	—	—	—	—	—	—	—	—	—	—	—	—
John Marshall	91	—	—	—	—	—	—	—	—	—	—	—	—
Joseph Story	64	—	—	—	—	—	—	—	—	—	—	—	—

NAMES NOT CHOSEN

	1900	1905	1910	1915	1920	1925	1930	1935	1940	1945	1950	1955	1960
John Peter Altgeld	—	—	—	—	—	—	—	—	—	—	—	3	1
John M. Becker	—	—	—	—	—	—	—	—	—	—	—	—	0
Joseph H. Choate	—	—	—	—	—	—	—	—	—	0	1	—	—
Thomas McIntyre Cooley	—	—	—	23	45	—	19	—	6	—	—	—	—
Oliver Ellsworth	10	15	13	3	2	—	—	—	—	—	—	—	—
William Maxwell Evarts	—	—	—	10	10	—	—	—	—	—	—	—	—
Stephen J. Field	—	—	—	—	1	—	—	—	—	—	—	—	—
Andrew Hamilton	—	—	—	—	—	—	—	—	—	—	—	—	0
John Marshall Harlan	—	—	—	—	—	—	—	—	—	—	—	1	—
Oliver Wendell Holmes, Jr.	—	—	—	—	—	—	—	—	—	—	—	—	57
Robert G. Ingersoll	—	—	—	—	—	—	—	3	2	0	0	5	0
William Johnson	—	—	—	—	—	—	0	—	—	—	—	—	—
L. Q. C. Lamar	—	—	—	—	2	—	—	—	—	—	—	—	—
Edward Livingston	14	9	12	4	4	—	—	—	—	—	—	—	—
Louis Marshall	—	—	—	—	—	—	—	—	—	—	—	—	1
Thomas J. O'Donnell	—	—	—	—	—	—	—	—	—	—	—	0	—
William Pinkney	—	—	—	—	2	—	—	—	—	—	—	—	—
John Rutledge	—	—	—	—	—	—	—	—	—	—	—	1	—
Lemuel Shaw	11	10	11	19	27	—	—	—	—	—	—	—	—
Roger Brooke Taney	17	13	13	6	5	—	—	—	22	3	—	2	0
Henry Wheaton	13	9	11	6	2	—	—	—	—	—	—	—	—
Edward Douglass White	—	—	—	—	—	—	—	—	—	—	—	—	0

XII — Statesmen

NAMES CHOSEN

	1900	1905	1910	1915	1920	1925	1930	1935	1940	1945	1950	1955	1960
John Adams	62	—	—	—	—	—	—	—	—	—	—	—	—
John Quincy Adams	48	60	—	—	—	—	—	—	—	—	—	—	—
Henry Clay	74	—	—	—	—	—	—	—	—	—	—	—	—
Grover Cleveland	—	—	—	—	35	—	—	77	—	—	—	—	—
Benjamin Franklin	94	—	—	—	—	—	—	—	—	—	—	—	—
Alexander Hamilton	—	—	—	70	—	—	—	—	—	—	—	—	—
Patrick Henry	39	46	44	47	57	—	—	—	—	—	—	—	—
Andrew Jackson	48	46	53	—	—	—	—	—	—	—	—	—	—
Thomas Jefferson	91	—	—	—	—	—	—	—	—	—	—	—	—
Abraham Lincoln	96	—	—	—	—	—	—	—	—	—	—	—	—
James Madison	49	56	—	—	—	—	—	—	—	—	—	—	—

XII—STATESMEN [*Continued*]

	1900	1905	1910	1915	1920	1925	1930	1935	1940	1945	1950	1955	1960
James Monroe	19	24	27	6	6	—	66	—	—	—	—	—	—
William Penn	—	—	—	—	11	44	58	83	—	—	—	—	—
Theodore Roosevelt	—	—	—	—	—	—	—	—	—	30	70	—	—
George Washington	97	—	—	—	—	—	—	—	—	—	—	—	—
Daniel Webster	96	—	—	—	—	—	—	—	—	—	—	—	—
Woodrow Wilson	—	—	—	—	—	—	—	—	—	—	77	—	—

NAMES NOT CHOSEN

	1900	1905	1910	1915	1920	1925	1930	1935	1940	1945	1950	1955	1960
Charles Francis Adams	4	6	20	7	5	—	—	—	—	—	—	—	—
Samuel Adams	33	26	41	37	42	58	32	13	14	2	—	1	1
Chester A. Arthur	—	—	—	—	—	—	—	—	0	—	—	0	—
Moses Austin	—	—	—	—	—	—	—	—	—	—	0	0	—
Stephen Fuller Austin	—	—	—	—	—	—	0	—	1	—	0	0	0
Judah Philip Benjamin	—	—	—	—	—	—	—	—	—	—	—	—	0
Thomas Hart Benton	16	12	15	1	1	—	—	—	—	—	—	0	0
John Bigelow	—	—	—	—	—	—	—	—	—	—	0	—	—
James Gillespie Blaine	—	12	14	0	2	—	—	—	3	—	0	0	—
Richard Bland	—	—	—	—	—	—	—	—	—	—	—	—	0
William Bradford	—	—	—	5	2	—	—	—	—	—	—	—	—
William Jennings Bryan	—	—	—	—	—	—	—	—	—	—	2	1	0
Aaron Burr	—	—	—	—	—	—	—	—	—	—	—	—	0
John Caldwell Calhoun	49	46	42	22	18	—	19	—	22	4	1	1	2
Charles Carroll	2	—	—	—	—	—	—	—	1	—	—	0	0
Lewis Cass	—	—	—	—	—	—	—	—	—	—	—	0	—
Salmon Portland Chase	13	14	9	1	1	—	—	—	—	—	—	—	—
John Clarke	—	—	—	—	—	—	—	—	1	—	—	—	—
DeWitt Clinton	8	14	15	2	0	—	—	—	2	—	0	—	—
George Clinton	—	—	—	—	—	—	—	—	—	—	—	0	—
Calvin Coolidge	—	—	—	—	—	—	—	—	—	—	—	—	0
John Warwick Daniel	—	—	—	—	—	—	—	—	—	—	—	—	0
Jefferson Davis	—	—	—	—	—	—	3	8	—	—	1	1	44
Edward Everett	—	9	20	0	0	—	—	—	—	0	—	—	—
Albert Gallatin	—	—	—	9	3	—	26	19	—	—	—	2	8
James Abram Garfield	7	11	13	0	3	—	2	—	—	—	—	—	—
George Goethals	—	—	—	—	—	—	—	—	—	—	—	2	0
John Hancock	12	13	31	4	6	—	—	—	—	—	—	0	0
John Hanson	—	—	—	—	—	—	—	—	3	—	—	—	—
Warren G. Harding	—	—	—	—	—	—	—	—	—	—	0	—	—
Townsend Harris	—	—	—	—	—	—	—	—	4	—	—	—	0
Benjamin Harrison	—	—	—	—	—	—	—	—	0	—	—	—	0
William Henry Harrison	—	—	—	—	—	—	—	—	4	—	—	0	0
John Hay	—	—	—	16	13	—	26	18	18	—	2	—	0
Rutherford B. Hayes	—	—	—	—	—	—	—	—	—	—	0	0	—
Samuel Houston	16	10	6	2	6	—	7	—	13	2	2	4	0
John Jay	25	26	36	30	33	59	24	9	22	3	1	1	0
Andrew Johnson	—	—	—	—	—	—	—	—	8	—	—	—	0
Lafayette	—	—	—	—	—	—	—	—	—	—	0	0	—
Robert M. LaFollette, Sr.	—	—	—	—	—	—	—	—	—	—	—	2	2
Richard Henry Lee	3	—	—	—	—	—	—	—	3	—	—	0	—

XII—STATESMEN [Continued]

	1900	1905	1910	1915	1920	1925	1930	1935	1940	1945	1950	1955	1960
Robert R. Livingston	3	10	7	0	1	—	—	—	—	—	—	—	—
Henry Cabot Lodge	—	—	—	—	—	—	—	—	—	—	—	0	—
Nathaniel Macon	—	—	—	—	—	—	—	—	—	—	0	—	—
William McKinley	—	—	—	—	9	—	1	—	4	0	0	0	0
George Mason	—	—	—	—	—	—	—	—	—	—	—	—	3
John Tyler Morgan	—	—	—	—	—	—	—	—	—	—	—	—	1
Justin Smith Morrill	—	—	—	—	—	—	—	—	—	—	—	—	3
Gouverneur Morris	7	—	—	—	—	—	1	—	5	—	0	—	0
Robert Morris	—	—	—	6	2	—	7	—	—	0	—	—	0
John Morton	—	—	—	—	—	—	—	—	—	—	—	0	—
J. Sterling Morton	—	—	—	—	—	—	—	—	—	—	0	0	—
Frederick A. C. Muhlenberg	—	—	—	—	—	—	—	—	—	—	—	0	—
James E. Oglethorpe	—	—	—	—	—	—	—	—	1	1	0	—	—
James Otis	4	—	—	—	—	9	1	—	—	—	—	—	—
Samuel W. Pennypacker	—	—	—	—	—	—	—	—	—	—	—	0	—
Charles Pinckney	—	—	—	—	—	—	—	—	1	—	—	—	—
Charles Cotesworth Pinckney	4	—	—	—	—	—	—	—	1	—	—	—	—
Thomas C. Platt	—	—	—	—	—	—	—	—	0	—	—	—	—
James K. Polk	—	—	—	—	—	—	—	—	—	—	—	1	2
Alexander Ramsey	—	—	—	—	—	—	—	—	—	—	0	—	—
Thomas Brackett Reed	—	—	—	—	1	—	—	—	—	—	—	—	—
Edmund Ross	—	—	—	—	—	—	—	—	—	—	—	—	0
Carl Schurz	—	—	—	—	—	—	—	—	14	—	0	2	1
William Henry Seward	25	27	31	7	1	—	3	—	—	—	0	—	2
James S. Sherman	—	—	—	—	—	—	—	—	—	—	—	—	—
Roger Sherman	5	12	12	2	1	—	—	—	—	—	—	0	—
Edwin McMasters Stanton	6	13	9	1	3	—	—	—	4	—	—	—	—
Alexander Hamilton Stephens	7	12	11	2	1	—	—	—	—	—	—	—	0
Thaddeus Stevens	—	—	—	—	—	—	—	—	—	—	0	0	—
Oscar Solomon Straus	—	—	—	—	—	—	—	—	—	—	—	—	0
John L. Sullivan	—	—	—	—	—	—	—	—	—	—	0	—	—
Charles Sumner	26	28	24	7	4	—	—	—	6	—	—	—	—
William Howard Taft	—	—	—	—	—	—	—	—	—	—	—	1	—
Samuel Jones Tilden	—	—	—	—	—	—	—	—	—	—	—	—	0
Daniel D. Tompkins	—	—	—	—	—	—	—	—	—	—	0	—	—
William B. Travis	—	—	—	—	—	—	—	—	—	—	—	0	0
Jonathan Trumbull	—	—	—	—	—	—	2	—	—	—	—	—	—
Thomas James Walsh	—	—	—	—	—	—	—	—	—	—	—	—	1
Brand Whitlock	—	—	—	—	—	—	—	—	—	—	—	—	0
William Collins Whitney	—	—	—	—	—	—	—	—	—	—	—	0	—
James Wilson	—	—	—	—	—	—	—	6	—	—	—	1	—
Anthony Winston	—	—	—	—	—	—	—	—	—	—	—	0	—
John Winthrop	—	—	—	—	—	—	—	—	—	—	—	—	0

XIII — Business Men and Philanthropists

NAMES CHOSEN

	1900	1905	1910	1915	1920	1925	1930	1935	1940	1945	1950	1955	1960
Peter Cooper	69	—	—	—	—	—	—	—	—	—	—	—	—
George Peabody	74	—	—	—	—	—	—	—	—	—	—	—	—

NAMES NOT CHOSEN

	1900	1905	1910	1915	1920	1925	1930	1935	1940	1945	1950	1955	1960
Philip D. Armour	—	—	—	—	—	—	—	—	—	0	—	0	—
John Jacob Astor	—	—	—	—	—	—	—	—	—	—	0	0	—
John Adam Beckley	—	—	—	—	—	—	—	—	—	0	—	—	—
Andrew Carnegie	—	—	—	—	—	—	—	—	—	10	23	49	65
William Colgate	—	—	—	—	—	—	—	—	—	—	—	0	—
Ezra Cornell	—	—	—	—	—	—	—	—	—	—	—	0	—
Anthony J. Drexel	—	—	—	—	—	—	—	—	—	—	—	0	—
James B. Duke	—	—	—	—	—	—	—	—	—	—	—	0	—
E. I. DuPont de Nemours	—	—	—	—	—	—	—	—	—	—	—	2	—
Thomas Clark Durant	—	—	—	—	—	—	0	—	—	—	—	—	—
George Eastman	—	—	—	—	—	—	—	—	—	—	—	—	1
John Evans	—	—	—	—	—	—	—	—	—	—	—	—	0
Cyrus Field	—	—	—	—	—	34	23	25	38	1	0	—	—
Marshall Field	—	—	—	—	5	—	—	—	—	0	—	0	—
Haley Fiske	—	—	—	—	—	—	—	—	—	—	—	0	—
Thomas Fitzsimmons	—	—	—	—	—	—	—	—	—	—	—	0	—
Henry Clay Frick	—	—	—	—	—	—	—	—	—	0	0	—	—
Stephen Girard	—	3	6	8	11	—	—	—	4	0	0	2	—
Edward H. Harriman	—	—	—	—	—	—	—	—	—	—	—	0	—
George Huntington Hartford	—	—	—	—	—	—	—	—	—	—	—	—	0
Philip Hone	—	—	—	—	—	—	—	—	—	0	—	—	—
Johns Hopkins	—	4	4	8	9	—	—	—	9	—	1	0	1
John McDonough	—	—	—	—	—	—	—	—	—	—	—	0	—
John Pierpont Morgan	—	—	—	—	—	—	—	—	10	—	—	0	—
Junius Spence Morgan	—	—	—	—	—	—	—	—	—	—	—	—	0
James W. Packard	—	—	—	—	—	—	—	—	—	—	—	0	—
William Patterson	—	—	—	—	—	—	—	—	—	—	—	0	—
Henrietta Howland Robinson	—	—	—	—	—	—	—	—	—	—	—	—	0
Haym Salomon	—	—	—	—	—	—	—	—	3	0	0	0	0
Samuel Slater	—	—	—	—	—	—	—	—	—	—	0	—	—
Leland Stanford	—	—	—	—	—	—	—	—	—	—	—	0	—
William Steinway	—	—	—	—	—	—	—	—	—	—	—	0	—
John B. Stetson	—	—	—	—	—	—	—	—	—	—	—	0	—
Edward R. Stettinius	—	—	—	—	—	—	—	—	—	—	—	0	—
Charles Lewis Tiffany	—	—	—	—	—	—	—	—	—	—	—	—	0
Gustavus Franklin Swift	—	—	—	—	—	—	—	—	—	0	—	—	—
Cornelius Vanderbilt	30	9	5	4	4	—	—	—	—	—	—	0	1
John Wanamaker	—	—	—	—	—	—	—	—	—	—	0	0	—
Joseph Wharton	—	—	—	—	—	—	—	—	—	1	0	—	—
Frank Winfield Woolworth	—	—	—	—	—	—	—	—	—	0	—	0	—
Elihu Yale	—	—	—	—	—	—	—	—	—	0	1	—	—

XIV — Artists

NAMES CHOSEN

	1900	1905	1910	1915	1920	1925	1930	1935	1940	1945	1950	1955	1960
Edwin Booth	—	—	30	38	48	85	—	—	—	—	—	—	—
Charlotte S. Cushman	13	39	45	53	—	—	—	—	—	—	—	—	—
Stephen Collins Foster	—	—	—	—	—	—	7	25	86	—	—	—	—
Edward Alexander MacDowell	—	—	—	—	5	—	—	29	38	36	9	53	72
Augustus Saint-Gaudens	—	—	—	—	67	—	—	—	—	—	—	—	—
Gilbert Charles Stuart	52	—	—	—	—	—	—	—	—	—	—	—	—
James A. McN. Whistler°	—	—	—	—	31	—	74	—	—	—	—	—	—

NAMES NOT CHOSEN

	1900	1905	1910	1915	1920	1925	1930	1935	1940	1945	1950	1955	1960
Thomas Ball	—	—	—	—	—	—	—	—	0	—	—	—	—
Paul Wayland Bartlett	—	—	—	—	—	—	—	—	—	0	—	—	—
George W. Bellows	—	—	—	—	—	—	—	—	—	—	1	—	0
George Caleb Bingham	—	—	—	—	—	—	—	—	—	—	0	—	—
Karl Bitter	—	—	—	—	—	—	—	—	0	—	—	—	—
Alfred Laurens Brennan	—	—	—	—	—	—	—	—	—	0	—	—	—
George Frederick Bristow	—	—	—	—	—	—	—	—	0	—	—	—	—
William M. Chase	—	—	—	—	—	—	—	—	0	0	—	—	—
Frederick Edwin Church	—	—	6	0	0	—	—	—	—	—	—	—	—
John Singleton Copley	33	25	28	27	12	36	49	38	52	9	—	—	—
Isadora Duncan	—	—	—	—	—	—	—	—	—	—	—	—	1
Thomas Eakins	—	—	—	—	—	—	—	—	—	—	—	2	3
Robert Feke	—	—	—	—	—	—	—	—	1	0	—	—	—
Edwin Forrest	6	—	—	—	0	—	—	3	—	—	—	—	—
John Frazee	—	—	—	—	—	—	—	—	0	—	—	—	—
Victor Herbert	—	—	—	—	—	—	—	—	—	—	1	4	5
Winslow Homer	—	—	—	—	—	—	—	—	—	—	—	20	26
Harriet Hosmer	—	—	—	5	12	—	—	—	—	—	—	—	—
George Inness	—	—	—	—	4	—	—	—	—	—	—	—	—
Joseph Jefferson	—	—	—	21	15	—	—	—	19	—	—	—	—
Rafael Joseffy	—	—	—	—	—	—	—	—	0	—	—	—	—
William Edgar Marshall	—	—	—	—	—	—	—	—	0	0	—	—	—
Lowell Mason	—	—	—	—	—	—	—	—	—	0	—	—	—
Thomas Nast	—	—	—	—	—	—	—	—	—	—	—	—	0
Ethelbert W. Nevin	—	—	—	—	—	—	—	—	—	—	0	—	—
Lillian Nordica	—	—	—	—	—	—	—	—	—	0	—	—	—
Frederick Law Olmsted	—	—	—	5	1	—	—	13	7	—	—	—	—
John Howard Payne	—	—	—	—	—	—	—	—	—	1	0	—	—
Maud Powell	—	—	—	—	—	—	—	—	—	0	—	—	—
Hiram Powers	36	15	7	4	2	—	—	—	—	—	0	—	—
James Pringle	—	—	—	—	—	—	—	—	0	—	—	—	—
Howard Pyle	—	—	—	—	—	—	—	—	3	—	—	—	—
John Rogers	—	—	—	—	—	—	—	0	—	—	0	—	—
Will Rogers	—	—	—	—	—	—	—	—	—	—	—	—	3
Charles W. Russell	—	—	—	—	—	—	—	—	—	—	—	1	—

XIV—ARTISTS [Continued]

	1900	1905	1910	1915	1920	1925	1930	1935	1940	1945	1950	1955	1960
John Singer Sargent	—	—	—	—	—	—	—	—	—	—	—	8	—
John Philip Sousa	—	—	—	—	—	—	—	—	—	—	—	—	0
Theodore Thomas	—	—	—	15	10	—	37	17	5	—	—	—	—
John Trumbull	—	—	—	—	—	—	—	—	—	0	—	—	—
John Quincy Adams Ward	—	—	—	—	6	—	—	4	1	—	—	—	—

*Whistler was eligible in 1920, but not in 1925.

XV—Naturalists

NAMES CHOSEN

NAMES NOT CHOSEN

	1900	1905	1910	1915	1920	1925	1930	1935	1940	1945	1950	1955	1960
Charles Edwin Bessey	—	—	—	—	—	—	—	—	—	—	0	—	—
Luther Burbank	—	—	—	—	—	—	—	—	—	—	—	42	37
John Burroughs	—	—	—	—	—	—	—	—	—	—	7	5	1
John Muir	—	—	—	—	—	—	—	—	4	1	2	4	3

XVI—Other Distinguished Men and Women Outside the Foregoing Classes

NAMES CHOSEN

NAMES NOT CHOSEN

	1900	1905	1910	1915	1920	1925	1930	1935	1940	1945	1950	1955	1960
Sarah Bache	—	7	12	1	2	—	—	—	—	—	—	—	—
Phineas Taylor Barnum	—	—	—	—	—	—	—	—	—	—	—	—	0
Clara Barton	—	—	—	—	—	—	—	—	12	1	5	13	5
Catherine Elizabeth Benson	—	—	—	—	—	—	—	—	—	—	—	—	0
Anna Ella Carroll	—	—	—	—	—	—	—	—	—	—	—	—	0
John Chapman (Johnny Appleseed)	—	—	—	—	—	—	—	—	—	0	—	—	0
Grace Dodge	—	—	—	—	—	—	—	—	1	—	—	—	—
Abner Doubleday	—	—	—	—	—	—	—	—	—	—	—	0	—
Edwin Laurentine Drake	—	—	—	—	—	—	—	—	—	—	0	—	—
Nathan Bedford Forrest	—	—	—	—	—	—	—	—	—	—	0	—	—
Jesse Root Grant	—	—	—	—	—	—	—	—	0	—	—	—	—
Josiah Hornblower	—	—	—	—	—	—	—	—	—	—	—	—	0
Sacagawea (of Shoshone)	—	—	—	—	—	—	—	—	—	—	—	—	0
Maggie Lena Walker	—	—	—	—	—	—	—	—	—	—	—	—	0
Florenz Ziegfeld	—	—	—	—	—	—	—	—	—	—	—	—	0

Sculptors of the Bronze Busts

IN THE HALL OF FAME

SCULPTOR	BUST
Adams, Herbert	John Marshall William Ellery Channing William Cullen Bryant Joseph Story
Aitken, Robert	Thomas Jefferson Daniel Webster Benjamin Franklin Henry Clay
Baker, Bryant	William Crawford Gorgas Thomas Jonathan "Stonewall" Jackson Thomas Alva Edison
Barthé, Richmond	Booker T. Washington
Beach, Chester	Peter Cooper Asa Gray Eli Whitney Samuel Finley Breese Morse Walt Whitman
Brewster, George T.	Robert Edward Lee
Brigham, Emma F.	Maria Mitchell (*replica*)
Calder, A. Stirling	John James Audubon William Penn
Ceracchi, Giuseppe	Alexander Hamilton (*replica*)
Clark, Allan	James Russell Lowell
Evans, Rudulph	John Greenleaf Whittier Henry Wadsworth Longfellow George Bancroft Grover Cleveland
Flanagan, John	Joseph Henry
Fraser, James Earle (*with* Thomas Hudson Jones)	Ulysses Simpson Grant Augustus Saint-Gaudens

Fraser, Laura Gardin	Gilbert Charles Stuart
	Mary Lyon
French, Daniel Chester	Edgar Allan Poe
	Ralph Waldo Emerson
	Phillips Brooks
	Nathaniel Hawthorne
Grafly, Charles	James Buchanan Eads
	Jonathan Edwards
	David Glasgow Farragut
	John Paul Jones
Grimes, Frances	Charlotte Saunders Cushman
	Emma Willard
Hancock, Walker Kirtland	Stephen Collins Foster
	Woodrow Wilson
Hoffman, Malvina	Thomas Paine
Hoerbst, Hans	Mark Hopkins (*replica*)
Houdon, Jean-Antoine	Robert Fulton (*replica*)
	George Washington (*replica*)
Howard, Cecil	Walter Reed
Humphreys, Albert	Samuel Langhorne Clemens
	[Mark Twain]
Huntington, Anna Hyatt	Louis Agassiz
Jones, Thomas Hudson	
(*with* James Earle Frazer)	Ulysses Simpson Grant
Keck, Charles	James Madison
	Patrick Henry
	Elias Howe
Kinney, Belle	Andrew Jackson
Lober, Georg	Theodore Roosevelt
Longman, Evelyn	Alice Freeman Palmer
MacMonnies, Frederick	John Lothrop Motley
	James Abbott McNeill Whistler
	Simon Newcomb
MacNeil, Hermon A.	Roger Williams
	Rufus Choate
	Francis Parkman
	James Monroe
McCartan, Edward	Washington Irving
Martineau, Stanley	Alexander Graham Bell
	Josiah Willard Gibbs

Mears, Helen Farnsworth	William Thomas Green Morton (*replica*)
Paramino, John Francis	John Adams
Polasek, Albin	Daniel Boone
Putnam, Brenda	Harriet Beecher Stowe
	Susan B. Anthony
Quattrocchi, Edmondo	George Westinghouse
Quinn, Edmond T.	Edwin Booth
	James Kent
	Oliver Wendell Holmes
	John Quincy Adams
Rhind, Massey	Henry Ward Beecher
Saint-Gaudens, Augustus	Abraham Lincoln (*replica*)
	William Tecumseh Sherman (*replica*)
Salvatore, Victor	James Fenimore Cooper
Schuler, Hans	George Peabody
	Sidney Lanier
Sievers, F. William	Matthew Fontaine Maury
Taft, Lorado	Frances Elizabeth Willard
Weinman, Adolph A.	Horace Mann

The Hall of Fame Art Committee: Donald De Lue, *Chairman;* Stanley Martineau, Michael Lantz, C. Paul Jennewein

The College of Electors

1960

Actor or Former University
or College Executives

Arthur S. Adams, D.C.
Raymond B. Allen, Cal.
J. Seelye Bixler, Me.
Sarah Gibson Blanding, N.Y.
Harvie Branscomb, Tenn.
William S. Carlson, Ohio
Oliver C. Carmichael, N.C.
Ben M. Cherrington, Col.
W. P. Clark, Mont.
*Robert C. Clothier, Pa.
Arthur H. Compton, Mo.
Bernice Brown Cronkhite, Mass.
G. L. Cross, Okla.
John S. Dickey, N.H.
*Harold W. Dodds, N.J.
Milton S. Eisenhower, Md.
*Frank L. Eversull, Ill.
Edwin B. Fred, Wis.
A. Whitney Griswold, Conn.
Virgil M. Hancher, Iowa
John A. Hannah, Mich.
Rufus C. Harris, La.
David D. Henry, Ill.
H. M. Ivy, Miss.
Barnaby C. Keeney, R.I.
Grayson Kirk, N.Y.
J. Howard Kramer, S.D.
Henry Noble MacCracken, N.Y.
Deane W. Malott, N.Y.
Willfred Mauck, Md.
Benjamin E. Mays, Ga.
James A. McCain, Kan.
Millicent C. McIntosh, N.Y.
John S. Millis, Ohio
J. L. Morrill, Minn.
Franklin D. Murphy, Kan.
Roy F. Nichols, Pa.

Theophilus S. Painter, Tex.
John E. Pomfret, Cal.
Nathan M. Pusey, Mass.
Homer P. Rainey, Col.
*Alexander G. Ruthven, Mich.
Robert Gordon Sproul, Cal.
Irvin Stewart, W. Va.
Samuel S. Stratton, Vt.
D. R. Theophilus, Idaho
Herman B Wells, Ind.
John C. West, N.D.
John D. Williams, Miss.
*Henry M. Wriston, R.I.

Historians or Professors
of History or Literature

Bruce Catton, N.Y.
*Guy Stanton Ford, D.C.
Allan Nevins, Cal.
James C. Olson, Neb.

Scientists

*Donald C. Balfour, Minn.
A. P. Black, Fla.
Detlev W. Bronk, N.Y.
Cecil W. Creel, Nev.
C. W. Mayo, Minn.
Robert Oppenheimer, N.J.
Fairfield Osborn, N.Y.
Jonas Edward Salk, Pa.
W. F. G. Swann, Pa.
J. C. Walker, Wis.

Authors, Editors, and Artists

Marian Anderson, Conn.
Robert B. Atwood, Alaska
Van Wyck Brooks, Conn.
John Dos Passos, Va.

*Stanly A. Easton, *Cal.*
Hermann Hagedorn, *N.Y.*
Howard Hanson, *N.Y.*
John Kieran, *Mass.*
Joseph Wood Krutch, *Ariz.*
Oliver La Farge, *N.Mex.*
*Walter Lippmann, *D.C.*
Henry R. Luce, *N.Y.*
Ralph McGill, *Ga.*
Hamilton Owens, *Md.*
*Clarence Poe, *N.C.*
Eugene C. Pulliam, *Ind.*
Helen Rogers Reid, *N.Y.*
Archibald Rutledge, *S.C.*
Carl Sandburg, *N.C.*
Deems Taylor, *N.Y.*
*Stark Young, *N.Y.*

Men and Women of Affairs

Bernard M. Baruch, *N.Y.*
*Arthur J. Brown, *Ohio*
*Cyrus S. Eaton, *Ohio*
Louis Finkelstein, *N.Y.*
*Harry Emerson Fosdick, *N.Y.*
William T. Gossett, *Mich.*
C. H. Greenewalt, *Del.*
Alfred M. Gruenther, *Neb.*
*Ralph Hayes, *Del.*
Henry T. Heald, *N.Y.*
August Heckscher, *N.Y.*
Henry Wise Hobson, *Ohio*
Paul G. Hoffman, *Col.*
John LaFarge, *N.Y.*
William Fisher Lewis, *Wash.*
Thurgood Marshall, *N.Y.*
Thomas W. Martin, *Ala.*
George Meany, *D.C.*
Reinhold Niebuhr, *N.Y.*
*Lewis Perry, *Mass.*
Eleanor Roosevelt, *N.Y.*
Alfred P. Sloan, Jr., *N.Y.*
Charles P. Taft, *Ohio*
*Owen D. Young, *N.Y.*

Actual or Former High Public Officials

Sherman Adams, *N.H.*
Robert B. Anderson, *Tex.*
*Percival P. Baxter, *Me.*
Ralph J. Bunche, *N.Y.*
James F. Byrnes, *S.C.*
Millard F. Caldwell, *Fla.*
LeRoy Collins, *Fla.*
John Sherman Cooper, *Ky.*
*L. W. Douglas, *Ariz.*
Marriner S. Eccles, *Utah*
Ralph E. Flanders, *Vt.*
Hiram L. Fong, *Hawaii*
*Felix Frankfurter, *D.C.*
J. W. Fulbright, *Ark.*
Frank P. Graham, *N.C.*
Herbert Hoover, *N.Y.*
Hubert H. Humphrey, *Minn.*
Jacob K. Javits, *N.Y.*
James R. Killian, Jr., *Mass.*
Walter J. Kohler, *Wis.*
Herbert H. Lehman, *N.Y.*
Neil H. McElroy, *Ohio*
James E. Murray, *Mont.*
Joseph C. O'Mahoney, *Wyo.*
Frederick A. Seaton, *Neb.*
Harold E. Stassen, *Pa.*
Adlai E. Stevenson, *Ill.*
Hatton W. Sumners, *Tex.*
*Henry A. Wallace, *N.Y.*
Arthur V. Watkins, *Utah*

*Actual or Former Justices,
National or State*

*Florence E. Allen, *Ohio*
*Learned Hand, *N.Y.*
Matthew W. Hill, *Wash.*
William J. Jameson, *Mont.*
John C. Knox, *N.Y.*
Charles L. Terry, Jr., *Del.*
Earl Warren, *Wash.*

The College of Electors
1900 through 1960

*Members of the College of Electors who have been elected to the Hall of Fame.

A	NUMBER OF ELECTIONS	PERIOD OF MEMBERSHIP
Adams, Arthur S.	3	1950 – 1960
Adams, George Burton	3	1910 – 1920
Adams, Henry Carter	3	1900 – 1910
Adams, Herbert	4	1930 – 1945
Adams, James Truslow	3	1935 – 1945
Adams, Sherman	2	1955 – 1960
Alderman, Edwin Anderson	7	1900 – 1930
Allen, Florence E.	5	1940 – 1960
Allen, Henry J.	2	1945 – 1950
Allen, Raymond B.	3	1950 – 1960
Anderson, Marian	1	1960
Anderson, Robert B.	1	1960
Andrews, Charles M.	5	1900 – 1920
Andrews, Roy Chapman	5	1940 – 1960
Angell, James B.	9	1900 – 1940
Atwood, Robert B.	1	1960
Aydelotte, Frank	4	1940 – 1955
B		
Babcock, Kendrick C.	2	1925 – 1930
Baker, Newton D.	2	1930 – 1935
Balfour, Donald Church	5	1940 – 1960
Bancroft, Joseph	1	1935
Barrows, John H.	1	1900
Bartch, George W.	2	1900 – 1905
Bartholomew, J. M.	1	1900
Baruch, Bernard M.	1	1960
Battle, George Gordon	2	1940 – 1945
Baxter, Percival P.	5	1940 – 1960
*Bell, Alexander Graham	2	1915 – 1920
Benton, Guy P.	3	1910 – 1920
Billings, John S.	3	1900 – 1910
Bixler, Julius S.	2	1955 – 1960
Bizzell, William Bennett	2	1935 – 1940
Black, Alvin P.	2	1955 – 1960
Black, Norman	2	1925 – 1930

	NUMBER OF ELECTIONS	PERIOD OF MEMBERSHIP
Blackmar, Frank W.	7	1900 – 1930
Blanding, Sarah Gibson	3	1950 – 1960
Blashfield, Edwin H.	3	1925 – 1935
Boardman, Mabel T.	6	1920 – 1945
Bole, James P.	2	1935 – 1940
Borah, William E.	1	1940
Bourne, Edward G.	2	1900 – 1905
Bourne, Henry E.	9	1900 – 1945
Bowman, Isaiah	3	1940 – 1950
Bowne, Bordon P.	2	1900 – 1905
Branscomb, Harvie	1	1960
Brantley, Theodore	5	1900 – 1920
Breaux, Joseph A.	2	1905 – 1910
Brewer, David J.	2	1900 – 1905
Bronk, Detlev W.	3	1950 – 1960
Brookings, Robert S.	3	1915 – 1925
Brooks, Van Wyck	3	1950 – 1960
Brown, Arthur J.	10	1915 – 1960
Brush, George J.	3	1900 – 1910
Bryan, William J.	1	1910
Buckley, James M.	4	1900 – 1915
Bullitt, William Marshall	5	1935 – 1955
Bunche, Ralph J.	3	1950 – 1960
Burgess, John W.	5	1900 – 1920
Burke, John	1	1935
Burnett, E. A.	1	1935
Burr, George L.	6	1910 – 1935
Burt, Struthers	5	1930 – 1950
Butler, Nicholas Murray	1	1935
Byrnes, James F.	1	1960
C		
Cable, George W.	2	1915 – 1920
Cabot, Hugh	2	1940 – 1945
Caldwell, F. Millard	2	1955 – 1960
Cammack, James W.	1	1955
Campbell, John	1	1900
Carlson, William H.	3	1950 – 1960
Carmichael, Oliver C.	2	1955 – 1960
Carnegie, Andrew	1	1910
Carroll, J. P.	1	1925
Catton, Bruce	1	1960
Cassoday, J. B.	2	1900 – 1905
Channing, Edward	6	1900 – 1930
Chaplin, W. S.	2	1900 – 1905
Cherrington, Ben Mark	4	1945 – 1960

	NUMBER OF ELECTIONS	PERIOD OF MEMBERSHIP
Choate, Joseph H.	2	1910 – 1915
Churchill, Winston	2	1915 – 1920
Clark, Bennett Champ	2	1935 – 1940
Clark, Walter	4	1905 – 1920
Clark, Wesley Plummer	2	1955 – 1960
*Cleveland, Grover	1	1900
Clifford, Cornelius C.	1	1935
Clothier, Robert C.	5	1940 – 1960
Coker, David R.	1	1935
Coleman, Norman F.	6	1930 – 1955
Collins, LeRoy	1	1960
Compton, Arthur H.	3	1950 – 1960
Conant, James Bryant	4	1935 – 1950
Connally, Tom T.	2	1945 – 1950
Cooper, John Sherman	1	1960
Corson, Dighton	2	1900 – 1905
Cortissoz, Royal	5	1925 – 1945
Crabites, Pierre	1	1940
Crawford, George Gordon	2	1930 – 1935
Crawford, William H.	9	1900 – 1940
Creel, Cecil Willis	2	1955 – 1960
Cronkhite, Bernice Brown	3	1950 – 1960
Cross, George L.	3	1950 – 1960
Cross, Wilbur L.	2	1940 – 1945
Cutting, Bronson	1	1935
D		
Dabney, Charles W.	8	1910 – 1945
Dabney, Richard H.	10	1900 – 1945
Davis, Harvey N.	1	1950
Davis, John W.	7	1925 – 1955
Day, James R.	5	1900 – 1920
Day, William R.	2	1915 – 1920
Denny, George H.	4	1940 – 1955
Dent, M. H.	1	1900
Dickey, John S.	1	1960
Dodd, William E.	2	1935 – 1940
Dodds, Harold Willis	6	1935 – 1960
Dolliver, Jonathan P.	1	1910
Dos Passos, John	2	1955 – 1960
Douglas, Lewis W.	5	1940 – 1960
Doyle, Michael Francis	2	1955 – 1960
Duniway, Clyde A.	9	1900 – 1940
Dunn, Gano	1	1950
DuPont, Alfred Victor	1	1950
Dykstra, Clarence K.	3	1940 – 1950

	NUMBER OF ELECTIONS	PERIOD OF MEMBERSHIP
E		
Easton, Stanly A.	8	1925 – 1960
Eaton, Cyrus S.	5	1940 – 1960
Eccles, Marriner S.	4	1945 – 1960
Edmunds, George F.	4	1900 – 1915
Egan, Maurice Francis	1	1920
Eggleston, Edward	1	1900
Eisenhower, Dwight D.	1	1950
Eisenhower, Milton S.	1	1960
Eliot, Charles W.	6	1900 – 1925
Erskine, John	4	1935 – 1950
Eversull, Frank Lissenden	5	1940 – 1960
F		
Fairbanks, Charles W.	3	1905 – 1915
Faircloth, William T.	1	1900
Faunce, W. H. P.	7	1900 – 1930
Finkelstein, Louis	1	1960
Finley, John Houstin	4	1920 – 1935
Fisher, Dorothy Canfield	1	1940
Fisher, George P.	2	1900 – 1905
Flanders, Ralph Edwards	2	1955 – 1960
Fling, Fred M.	7	1900 – 1930
Fong, Hiram L.	1	1960
Foote, Mary Hallock	4	1905 – 1920
Forbes, W. Cameron	6	1930 – 1955
Ford, Guy Stanton	5	1940 – 1960
Fosdick, Harry Emerson	7	1930 – 1960
Foster, John W.	2	1910 – 1915
Foster, William Trufant	7	1920 – 1950
Foulke, William Dudley	1	1920
Frankfurter, Felix	5	1940 – 1960
Fred, Edwin B.	3	1950 – 1960
Freeman, Douglas S.	1	1950
Freeman, James E.	1	1940
Fulbright, J. W.	2	1955 – 1960
Fuller, Melville W.	3	1900 – 1910
G		
Gaines, Reuben R.	2	1900 – 1905
Gabbert, William H.	1	1905
Gary, Elbert H.	3	1915 – 1925
Gates, George A.	1	1900
Gilbert, Cass	2	1925 – 1930
Gilder, Richard Watson	2	1900 – 1905

181

	NUMBER OF ELECTIONS	PERIOD OF MEMBERSHIP
Glasgow, Ellen	5	1925 – 1945
Goethels, George W.	3	1915 – 1925
Gonzales, William E.	2	1930 – 1935
Goodnow, Frank J.	2	1930 – 1935
Gossett, William T.	1	1960
Graham, Frank P.	3	1950 – 1960
Grant, Frederick D.	1	1910
Greenewalt, Crawford H.	2	1955 – 1960
Griswold, A. Whitney	1	1960
Gruenther, Alfred M.	1	1960
Gustavson, Reuben G.	1	1950
H		
Hadley, Arthur T.	7	1900 – 1930
Hagedorn, Hermann	2	1955 – 1960
Hale, Edward Everett	2	1900 – 1905
Hale, George Ellery	1	1920
Hancher, Virgil M.	3	1950 – 1960
Hand, Learned	5	1940 –1960
Hannah, John A.	1	1960
Hanson, Howard	2	1955 – 1960
Harris, Rufus C.	4	1945 – 1960
Harrison, Charles C.	6	1900 – 1925
Hart, Albert B.	9	1900 – 1940
Hayes, Ralph	5	1940 – 1960
Hazard, Caroline	9	1905 – 1945
Hazelrig, James H.	1	1900
Hazen, Charles Downer	1	1940
Heald, Henry T.	1	1960
Heckscher, August	1	1960
Henry, David D.	1	1960
Herrick, Myron T.	3	1915 – 1925
Hewett, Edgar Lee	2	1940 – 1945
Hibben, John Grier	4	1915 – 1930
Higginson, Thomas W.	3	1900 – 1910
Hill, Albert Ross	1	1910
Hill, David Jayne	2	1925 – 1930
Hill, David Spence	6	1925 – 1950
Hill, James J.	1	1915
Hill, Joseph M.	1	1905
Hill, Matthew William	2	1955 – 1960
Hinsdale, Burke A.	1	1900
Hobby, Oveta Culp	1	1955
Hobson, Henry Wise	1	1960
Hobson, John P.	2	1905 – 1910

	NUMBER OF ELECTIONS	PERIOD OF MEMBERSHIP
Hoffman, Paul G.	2	1955 – 1960
Holland, Ernest O.	5	1930 – 1950
Holt, Hamilton	6	1925 – 1950
Hoover, Herbert	2	1955 – 1960
Hopkins, Ernest Martin	1	1920
Hughes, Charles Evans	7	1915 – 1945
Hume, Alfred	4	1935 – 1950
Humphrey, Hubert H.	1	1960
Hunt, Charles Warren	3	1900 – 1910
Huntington, Archer M.	6	1930 – 1955
Hurst, John F.	1	1900
Hutchins, Harry B.	2	1925 – 1930
Hyde, William De W.	4	1900 – 1915

I

Ivy, H. M.	2	1955 – 1960

J

James, Edmund J.	1	1910
Jameson, John F.	5	1900 – 1920
Jameson, William J.	2	1955 – 1960
Javits, Jacob K.	1	1960
Jesse, Richard Henry	1	1905
Jessup, Walter A.	2	1935 – 1940
Johnson, Allen	1	1930
Johnson, Charles S.	1	1955
Johnson, David Bancroft	2	1920 – 1925
Johnson, Hugh S.	2	1935 – 1940
Johnson, Lillian W.	1	1905
Johnson, Robert Underwood	2	1910 – 1915
Jones, Ira B.	1	1910
Jordan, David Starr	7	1900 – 1930
Judson, Harry P.	6	1900 – 1925

K

Kaempffert, Waldemar	2	1950 – 1955
Kane, Matthew J.	3	1910 – 1920
Keeney, Barnaby C.	1	1960
Keith, James	1	1900
Keller, Helen	5	1935 – 1955
Kieran, John F.	3	1950 – 1960
Killian, James R., Jr.	1	1960

	NUMBER OF ELECTIONS	PERIOD OF MEMBERSHIP
Kirk, Grayson	2	1955 – 1960
Kirkland, J. H.	8	1900 – 1935
Knox, John C.	3	1950 – 1960
Kohler, Walter J.	1	1960
Kramer, J. Howard	1	1960
Krutch, Joseph Wood	1	1960

L

LaFarge, John	1	1960
LaFarge, Oliver	3	1950 – 1960
LaFollette, Robert M.	1	1950
Lamont, Thomas W.	4	1930 – 1945
Lawrence, Ernest O.	2	1950 – 1955
LeConte, Joseph	1	1900
Lee, Umphrey	1	1955
Lehman, Herbert H.	1	1960
Lewis, William Fisher	2	1955 – 1960
Lincoln, Robert Todd	3	1910 – 1920
Lindsey, Ben	1	1925
Lippmann, Walter	6	1935 – 1960
Little, Arthur D.	2	1930 – 1935
Lore, Charles B.	1	1905
Low, Seth	4	1900 – 1915
Lowell, Abbott Lawrence	5	1910 – 1930
Luce, Henry R.	1	1960

MC

McBride, Katharine	1	1950
McCain, James A.	3	1950 – 1960
McCall, Samuel W.	1	1920
McClellan, Thomas N.	1	1905
McCormick, Anne O'Hare	4	1935 – 1950
McCormick, Samuel Black	4	1910 – 1925
McCulloch, Edgar A.	5	1910 – 1930
McElroy, Neil H.	2	1955 – 1960
McElroy, Robert	4	1935 – 1950
McGill, Ralph	1	1960
McIntosh, Millicent C.	3	1950 – 1960
McKelway, St. Clair	3	1900 – 1910
McLaughlin, Andrew C.	10	1900 – 1945
McMaster, John Bach	6	1905 – 1930
McPherson, John H. T.	11	1900 – 1950
McVey, Frank L.	3	1940 – 1950
McWhorter, Henry C.	1	1905

	NUMBER OF ELECTIONS	PERIOD OF MEMBERSHIP
M		
MacClellan, Thomas N.	1	1900
MacCracken, Henry Noble	3	1950 – 1960
MacCracken, John Henry	6	1920 – 1945
Malott, Deane W.	2	1955 – 1960
Manning, Richard I.	1	1930
Marburg, Theodore	5	1925 – 1945
Marshall, George C.	1	1950
Marshall, Thurgood	1	1960
Martin, Edward S.	3	1925 – 1935
Martin, Thomas W.	1	1960
Masters, Howard Russell	1	1955
Mather, Samuel	1	1930
Mauck, Willfred	2	1955 – 1960
Mayo, Charles H.	4	1920 – 1935
Mayo, C. W.	2	1955 – 1960
Mayo, William J.	3	1925 – 1935
Mays, Benjamin E.	2	1955 – 1960
Meany, George	1	1960
Melchers, Gari	1	1930
Merriam, John C.	5	1925 – 1945
Millay, Edna St. Vincent	4	1935 – 1950
Miller, Charles Ransom	1	1920
Millikan, Robert A.	5	1930 – 1950
Millis, John S.	3	1950 – 1960
Mills, Abbot L.	1	1925
Mims, Edwin	4	1940 – 1955
Moore, F. A.	2	1910 – 1915
Morgan, D. E.	1	1910
Morrill, James L.	2	1955 – 1960
Morris, Harrison S.	6	1925 – 1950
Morse, Anson D.	4	1900 – 1915
Morton, Henry	1	1900
Mott, John R.	9	1915 – 1955
Mount, Wallace	2	1905 – 1910
Murphy, Franklin D.	2	1955 – 1960
Murray, James E.	4	1945 – 1960
Myers, Philip V.	1	1900
N		
Nash, George W.	1	1940
Neely, Matthew M.	3	1945 – 1955
Nevins, Allen	3	1950 – 1960

	NUMBER OF ELECTIONS	PERIOD OF MEMBERSHIP
Newbranch, Harvey E.	4	1940 – 1955
*Newcomb, Simon	1	1905
Nichols, F. T.	1	1900
Nichols, Roy F.	1	1960
Nicholson, John R.	1	1900
Nicholson, Meredith	6	1920 – 1945
Niebuhr, Reinhold	2	1955 – 1960
Norcross, F. H.	9	1910 – 1950
Norlin, George	3	1930 – 1940
Northrop, Cyrus	4	1905 – 1920
Norval, T. L.	1	1900

O		
Ochs, Adolph S.	2	1930 – 1935
Olson, James C.	2	1955 – 1960
O'Mahoney, Joseph C.	2	1955 – 1960
Oppenheimer, Robert	3	1950 – 1960
Osborn, Henry Fairfield	6	1910 – 1935
Osborn, Fairfield	3	1950 – 1960
Owens, J. Hamilton	2	1955 – 1960

P		
Painter, Theophilus S.	3	1950 – 1960
*Palmer, Alice F.	1	1900
Parker, John M.	3	1925 – 1935
Patterson, Grove Hiram	1	1955
Pennewill, James	4	1910 – 1925
Perry, Bliss	3	1920 – 1930
Perry, James De Wolf	3	1935 – 1945
Perry, Lewis	8	1925 – 1960
Phelps, William Lyon	4	1925 – 1940
Pickering, Edward C.	4	1900 – 1915
Poe, Clarence	8	1925 – 1960
Pomfret, John E.	3	1950 – 1960
Pope, Young J.	1	1905
Porter, Horace	3	1910 – 1920
Post, George E.	2	1900 – 1905
Potter, Charles N.	6	1900 – 1925
Pratt, Ruth Baker	6	1930 – 1955
Pulitzer, Joseph	1	1945
Pulliam, Eugene C.	1	1960
Pusey, Nathan M.	2	1955 – 1960
Putnam, Herbert	10	1910 – 1955

	NUMBER OF ELECTIONS	PERIOD OF MEMBERSHIP
R		
Rainey, Homer P.	4	1945 – 1960
Raymond, Rossiter W.	4	1900 – 1915
Reid, Helen Rogers	3	1950 – 1960
Reid, Whitelaw	3	1900 – 1910
Remsen, Ira	5	1905 – 1925
Repplier, Agnes	4	1925 – 1940
Reynolds, John Hugh	3	1940 – 1950
Rhodes, James F.	6	1900 – 1925
Riggs, Theodore F.	3	1945 – 1955
Riley, James Whitcomb	1	1915
Robertson, Alice M.	2	1925 – 1930
Robinson, Joseph T.	1	1935
Rockefeller, Abby A.	2	1940 – 1945
Rogers, Edith Nourse	4	1930 – 1945
Rogers, Henry Wade	6	1900 – 1925
Rohde, Ruth Bryan	1	1950
Roosevelt, Eleanor	1	1960
*Roosevelt, Theodore	1	1900
Root, Elihu	4	1920 – 1935
Roper, Daniel C.	1	1940
Rowell, John W.	2	1905 – 1910
Ruthven, Alexander G.	6	1935 – 1960
Rutledge, Archibald H.	4	1945 – 1960
Ryan, James Hugh	3	1935 – 1945
S		
Sabin, Florence R.	3	1935 – 1945
Salk, Jonas Edward	1	1960
Salmon, Lucy Maynard	5	1905 – 1925
Schaff, David S.	1	1900
Seaton, Frederick A.	1	1960
Sedgwick, Henry D.	4	1935 – 1950
Seerley, Henry	3	1920 – 1930
Shahan, Thomas J.	7	1900 – 1930
Shaw, Albert	10	1900 – 1945
Sheehan, Thomas J.	1	1920
Sheppard, Maurice	1	1920
Sheppard, Morris	6	1915 – 1940
Sheppard, Robert D.	1	1900
Sherman, Stuart P.	1	1925
Sherwin, John C.	1	1905
Showerman, Grant	3	1925 – 1935
Sills, Kenneth C. M.	7	1925 – 1955

	NUMBER OF ELECTIONS	PERIOD OF MEMBERSHIP
Sloane, William M.	6	1900 – 1925
Smith, Edward Grandison	2	1935 – 1940
Smoot, Reed	4	1925 – 1940
Snyder, Franklyn B.	2	1950 – 1955
Sproul, Robert A.	2	1950 – 1955
Sproul, Robert Gordon	1	1960
Starrett, Helen Ekin	2	1915 – 1920
Stassen, Harold E.	3	1950 – 1960
Start, Charles M.	1	1900
Stedman, E. C.	2	1900 – 1905
Stevenson, Adlai E.	1	1960
Stewart, Irvin	3	1950 – 1960
Stimson, Henry L.	2	1940 – 1945
Stoddard, George D.	2	1950 – 1955
Stone, Melville E.	2	1920 – 1925
Stratton, Samuel S.	2	1955 – 1960
Strauss, Oscar S.	3	1915 – 1925
Sumners, Hatton W.	4	1945 – 1960
Suzzallo, Henry	3	1920 – 1930
Swain, George F.	7	1900 – 1930
Swann, William F. G.	4	1945 – 1960

T

Taft, Charles P.	3	1950 – 1960
Taft, Robert A.	1	1950
Taft, William Howard	2	1915 – 1920
Taylor, Deems	2	1955 – 1960
Taylor, James H.	1	1905
Taylor, James M.	4	1900 – 1915
Taylor, Robert F.	6	1900 – 1925
Terry, Charles L., Jr.	2	1955 – 1960
Thayer, William Roscoe	1	1920
Theophilus, D. R.	1	1960
Thomas, M. Carey	4	1900 – 1915
Thompson, Dorothy	4	1940 – 1955
Thwing, Charles F.	8	1900 – 1935
Tucker, William J.	4	1900 – 1915
Tupper, Frederick	5	1925 – 1945
Tyler, Moses Coit	1	1900

U

Underwood, Oscar W.	1	1925
Updegraff, Milton	3	1925 – 1935
Upson, Anson Judd	1	1900

	NUMBER OF ELECTIONS	PERIOD OF MEMBERSHIP
V		
Van Dyke, Henry	4	1915 – 1930
Van Hise, Charles R.	2	1910 – 1915
Vincent, George E.	5	1930 – 1950
W		
Walcott, Charles D.	5	1905 – 1925
Walker, John Charles	2	1955 – 1960
Wallace, Henry A.	5	1940 – 1960
Walsh, Thomas J.	1	1930
Wanamaker, John	2	1915 – 1920
Warner, Charles Dudley	1	1900
Warren, Charles	3	1940 – 1950
Warren, Earl	1	1960
Warren, Henry K.	3	1925 – 1935
Washburn, George	3	1900 – 1910
Watkins, Arthur V.	1	1960
Watterson, Henry	2	1915 – 1920
Welch, William H.	7	1900 – 1930
Wells, Herman B	3	1950 – 1960
West, John C.	3	1950 – 1960
West, Willis M.	2	1900 – 1905
White, Andrew D.	4	1900 – 1915
White, William Allen	4	1925 – 1940
Whiting, Charles S.	3	1910 – 1920
Whitlock, Brand	2	1925 – 1930
Wickersham, George W.	1	1930
Williams, John D.	3	1950 – 1960
Williams, John Sharp	4	1915 – 1930
Williams, Talcott	1	1925
Wilmer, William H.	2	1930 – 1935
Wilson, Edmund B.	1	1935
*Wilson, Woodrow	1	1900
Charles E. Wolverton	2	1900 – 1905
Wood, Leonard	2	1920 – 1925
Woodberry, George Edward	4	1915 – 1930
Woods, Thomas H.	1	1900
Woodward, Robert S.	4	1905 – 1920
Woolley, Mary E.	9	1905 – 1945
Wriston, Henry M.	5	1940 – 1960
Y		
Young, Newton C.	1	1905
Young, Owen D.	7	1930 – 1960
Young, Stark	6	1935 – 1960

Donors of Busts

191

Principal Speakers at Dedication Ceremonies